Human
Like
Me, Jesus

**PRAYERS
WITH NOTES ON THE
HUMANISTIC REVOLUTION
BY**

Malcolm Boyd

SIMON AND SCHUSTER · NEW YORK

SECOND PRINTING

SBN 671-21023-8
LIBRARY OF CONGRESS CATALOG CARD NUMBER: 71-159125
DESIGNED BY IRVING PERKINS
MANUFACTURED IN THE UNITED STATES OF AMERICA
PRINTED BY MURRAY PRINTING CO., FORGE VILLAGE, MASS.
BOUND BY H. WOLFF BOOK MFG. CO., INC., NEW YORK, N.Y.

This book contains certain material from pieces by the author that originally appeared in the following publications: *Defiance #2*, the quarterly published by Paperback Library; *The Critic* magazine; *The New York Times*; *The Detroit Free Press*; *The Yale Daily News*; *The National Catholic Reporter*; *Free to Live, Free to Die* and *My Fellow Americans*, both published by Holt, Rinehart and Winston.

The author gratefully acknowledges permission to quote from *Whose Heaven, Whose Earth?* by Thomas and Marjorie Melville, copyright © 1971 by Alfred A. Knopf, Inc., and from *Sexual Politics*, by Kate Millett, copyright © 1970 by Doubleday and Company, Inc. Occasionally he quotes briefly from other authors and in each case gives credit in the text itself.

TO MY BROTHERS AND SISTERS
ON THE MARATHON RUN

Contents

Introduction

W<small>HY</small> have I chosen to write prayers in the midst of a period marked by secular rather than religious definitions of life?

Human Like Me, Jesus, is an affirmation of three beliefs that are central to my life. The first belief is that the humanness I share with other people links us together with an iron strength that stands against all separation, all ghettos, all apartheid. The second belief is that my own humanness can never be taken away from me, either by a form of dehumanization seeking to crush me, or by tragic expressions of anti-life taking root within my own occasional feelings of frustration and despair. The third belief is that Jesus shares a common bond of humanity with all other people and myself. So Jesus illumines human life with holiness, rendering indissoluble what we call "the sacred" and "the secular."

Although some people hate organized religion or are indifferent to it, they do not (I believe) hate prayer or utterly shun what it implies—another dimension to life. Most people seem to be open to experiences of mystery,

9

sacrifice and celebration. There is widespread awareness of a human need for what is holy. In his book *A Rumor of Angels*, Peter Berger has spoken of "the capacity for ecstasy" as "any experience of stepping outside the taken-for-granted reality of everyday life, any openness to the mystery that surrounds us on all sides."

What is prayer?

Prayer, in my experience, is a creedal statement, not simply a petition. It is saying the creed of one's belief. For example, I find myself saying "I *want* to stand with the power of love, not that of killing; I *want* to stand with the power of reconciliation, not that of hate."

Prayer is truth; it is naming realities.

Prayer is asking honest questions.

Prayer can be two people talking together—or sharing silence—in mutually accepted openness and responsibility.

Prayer is not escapism and a turning away from other people and life, hence from God.

Prayer is affirmation of God's presence and love, and therefore the presence and meaning of human relationships. As affirmation, it is opening up one's life, moving outside the ghetto of self into concrete situations calling for compassion, sensitivity and mercy.

Prayer is awareness of mystery.

Prayer is sharing a vision of possibilities; it is communication.

Prayer is longing for new life as a prerequisite for its emergence in a perhaps wholly unexpected form.

Prayer is open participation in living.

Prayer is trying to love.

Prayer undergirds the humanistic revolution, even when it is not called prayer or uttered or acknowledged.

MALCOLM BOYD

Los Angeles, California
January 25, 1971

I

Prayers
for
Humans

PRAYERS OF
PERSONAL
IDENTITY

The inky prophecies of today's newspaper are gloomy, Jesus.

But I don't want to be dismayed by what appears hard or even hopeless.

I want to celebrate life.

Blood flows through my veins. Rain falls, Lord. Waters surge through the earth.

I know that the sun is up, Jesus, even when it is hidden by low gray clouds.

I know that the wind is here, even when it is so still. Look! A leaf trembles on that tree.

I can see yellows, reds, blues, greens, black and white.

Love. It is all around me. Sometimes it is called hate.

I feel like singing, smelling, looking, biting, laughing, tasting, crying, painting, walking, dancing, running . . .

Living, Jesus.

Who am I, Jesus?

I know there is a face, a smile, and a frown. There is passion, a residue of rage, and an icy capacity to withdraw. There is the familiar body, the uncharted mind, and the chameleon performing as a clown.

I know there is a tenderness, a warmth, and a biting revenge that reacts to real or imaginary hurt. There is the man-woman, the child, and the indelible image of God that calls to me in what I know as a conscience. There is a hunger that is insatiable, a thirst that burns and gnaws, and a hard selfishness that can be viciously cruel.

I know there is a vaulting ambition, a complex drive that will not let me rest, and a laziness made for a summer's day. There is an idealism that can startle my self-interest, a sense of duty that can suffocate my ticklish inclinations toward abandon, and a ruthless sense of self-sovereignty that can arrogantly try to bluff even Almighty God.

I know there is a cultivated self-sufficiency, a suicidal loneliness, and a dreaded anxiety. There is a personal history with tears and laughter, a public life, and a being so vulnerable that it can be smashed into pieces like a glass.

What is there in me of holiness, Jesus? What is there within me possessing hidden life that cannot be broken or burned or obliterated? What is there of me that is love, Lord?

You became human, Jesus. As a man you experienced loneliness, anger, joy, depression and hope.

Thank you for being human like me, Jesus.

I remember one night when I was a child, Jesus.

The soft light in the hallway seemed to flicker. There were footsteps on the stairs. My heart pounded. The footsteps were heavy—one, two, one, two. They came to the head of the stairs outside my room. It was the stout woman who had been hired to stay with me while my parents went out to the theater.

I was afraid of her. I knew that she did not like me. She treated me kindly when my parents were with us, but showed a cold hostility when we were alone. What did she want? Now the sound of footsteps ended. The silence was distressing. I must act as if I were asleep. I dared not move my eyelids or any part of my body. My back itched. My left leg felt as if it had a cramp.

The footsteps began again, creaking on the floor as they approached my bed. The stout woman stood by the side of the bed. I wanted to cry out, leap from my sheets and blankets, and run toward the door, but I knew it would be of no use. She would catch me. She must be looking down at my body in the long silence. Was she going to cook me in a great stew and eat me? She would tell my father and mother, when they came home, that I had run away. They would believe her and the terrible injustice would stand. No. No. Don't let her do this to me. I heard her footsteps on the bedroom floor. She was going away. She had decided not to cook me now but wait until later. Her footsteps were going down the stairs.

I must have fallen asleep. Suddenly, as if they had just begun speaking, two voices broke into my hearing. They were angry. I listened harder. They belonged to my father and mother. I almost jumped out of my bed to run into their room. I was happy that they had come home. The stout woman must have gone away. I was safe again.

But the anger in their voices warned me. I lay still in my bed, listening. I could not hear what words they were saying to each other. Then my mother said that she could not stand it any longer. My father swore at her. I heard a crash. What had happened? Was one of them hurt? I heard a door slam, and there was silence in the next room except for my mother's crying. The next morning I saw what had crashed. It was the glass covering a photograph of my father that always stood on their dresser.

All the next day the mood in the house was ominous. No one talked. I was treated as a child who did not know what had happened. That night my father and mother talked to me at the dinner table. They were going to separate, my mother said. That meant they would not live together anymore. My father took me up on his lap to hold me. He said they both wanted me to be happy. Would I decide which one of them I wanted to live with?

The next day, running in the ocean waves at the beach, with the sand between my toes, in my eyes and mouth, I felt that my heart had closed in on itself.

How much can a child understand, Jesus?

What is effectiveness, Jesus?

Some people place it ahead of honesty. But without honesty, wouldn't something just appear on the surface to be effective? I mean, it would really be a failure, Lord.

Success and failure seem to be badly misunderstood, don't they? They are judged by outward appearances instead of inner realities. I have felt my deepest failure at moments when people said I was a success, Lord. I have felt fulfilled and successful as a human being when I was most severely judged to be a failure.

You have taught us, Jesus, that a person can gain the whole world and lose his soul. This seems to be true for whole nations and societies too. Have we ever really heard what you were saying, Lord?

I envy someone, Jesus.

He is also someone whom I respect. It is just that he seems to be a better person than I am. He is gifted, kind, compassionate, patient and much more productive than I. He receives public acclaim in a situation where I have done as much work and am not thanked at all.

Why can't I accept his superiority gracefully, Lord? Why do I engage in this unprofitable and mean exercise of making comparisons between myself and him?

The feeling of envy cuts into my soul like acid eating flesh. I am burning and writhing under the pain, Jesus. The very existence of this person has become an irrational and insatiable threat to my being. Why am I so weak? Why am I so evil?

Help me to love the person whom I envy, Lord. Help me to love myself.

I was playing hopscotch around the center core of my life, Lord.

And before I knew it, I was consuming alcohol with the fervor of an addict. I set out to extinguish my fires, but they burned all the more brightly. I attended jet-set parties where waiters handed everybody a lethal new Martini, swimming luxuriantly in a clear glass, every eight minutes. I counted, Jesus.

I drank in neighborhood bars, those chummy, intimate, subdued places where quiet manners obscured the alcoholic brew that was churning inside their patrons' stomachs and heads.

At parties my friends gave I drank past the danger mark until I discovered that I had angrily broken a glass or accusingly insulted a fellow guest. Nice party, Sally! Great time, Danny! I stopped, Lord. Oh, I still take a drink, but I am not putting out fires. I have learned that fire is only fire.

Thanks for helping me to look deeply into that center core of my life, Jesus. Thanks for helping me to accept myself.

I feel detached from myself right now, Jesus.

It seems there are maybe four parts of me, or twelve, or thirty. Am I a simple schizoid or a whole complex pattern?

Someone asked me how I live with loneliness, Lord. Lone-li-ness. It seemed to me the alternative would be to die with it.

In this moment I am here, and there, and over *there*, and back *here*. I am interestingly fragmented, Jesus. I am in the present, the past, and the future. I am yellow and red and white and black and brown. I am Chinese in the thirteenth century, San Franciscan in the twenty-second, and Hun in the sixth. I am Babylonian. I am Assyrian. I am Chicagoan. I am Parisian. The human experience is splendid fun today, Jesus.

Once I thought that I could be a hero, Jesus.

Advancing against the enemy on a warrior's charger, with a mighty sword in my hand, I would uphold purity and justice against decadence and tyranny.

If a mere person lurked inside my hero's image, he must be denied, disciplined—flogged into submission, if need be—and forgotten. As a hero I realized that I would be lonely, Lord, even in the midst of convivial community, for I knew that I could never relax my role.

I could be king or president, messiah or bishop, general or statesman; they were heroes.

Then, one day, Jesus, I realized that I did not want to be a hero.

I cannot comprehend death, Jesus.

Will I be alive one moment, with all the submarine mechanism working, valves grinding, doors inside opening and closing—my dreams and hopes, plans and memories, fully charged with energy—and then, the next moment, will it all stop?

I don't know if I want to die or not, Lord.

Is life after death livable? I wonder if the intellect is respected, the arts flourish, there is at least a modicum of political integrity, and people love one another.

It scares me sometimes to be very serious about death, Lord. I would like to laugh about it too. Jesus, help me to understand what it is all about.

I have masqueraded as many things, Jesus.

Wasn't it easier, when I stepped outside the front door
of my house, to meet the needs of others by becoming
what they wished me to be? I was sad, I was gay. I
listened attentively, I spoke in words of wisdom. I was
humble and dutiful, I was proud and commanding. I
asked myself, Doesn't love require this?

All of us have played roles for such a long time. Yet
we are humans, Lord. If we did not so fiercely hold to our
roles, and obstinately imprison each other inside them,
we might learn to understand each other. Do you feel
we might even learn how to be compassionate, Jesus?

PRAYERS

FOR

LIBERATION

Why can't we permit the liberation of people and living things, Jesus?

Why can't we permit our own liberation?

"The universe has consciousness," the young Chicano told me.

"But the world is now uninhabitable. Man is acting fiercely against the consciousness of the universe."

It seems to me that we have a deadly definition of gods, Lord. We feel that to be a god is to ride roughshod over the earth, make decisions capriciously, act without feeling, and try to create terror in other people. We feel that to be a god is to claim the whole earth, and all of life within it, for our own use and destruction.

Could we start acting like humans, Jesus?

She feels that she has simply been programmed all of her life, Jesus.

What did it mean to be a woman? To her it meant an absence of equal opportunities, a sex role that became cloying, prescribed duties as a wife and a mother, social definitions of what she should legitimately feel and do in her life, rigidly imposed restrictions, contrasted with her husband's open sexual freedom outside their marriage, and a sense of dependence and powerlessness that has left her finally with a feeling of suppressed rage.

She is in her forties. She wants a freedom for the rest of her life that she has never known. She wants to break outside all categories that limit the full expression of her humanity.

How can she get outside the role she finds herself in, Jesus?

What is celebration, Jesus?

So many people call for props when they think of it—
lights, candles, incense, robes. They call for a crowd of
people—movement, density, bodies, choreography. They
demand music. But aren't they performing, Lord? If they
are playing roles, isn't it possible that celebration eludes
them?

It seems to me that celebration is being free. Being
one's own self, not trapped in a performance. Behaving
naturally and letting one's weakness show, and being
loved for oneself.

Power staggers my imagination, Jesus.

For example, Americans make up 6 percent of the world's population, yet America consumes 53 percent of the world's nonrenewable natural resources each year.

The United States nuclear arsenal contains 1,000 Minuteman missiles located within the country. Each one is equipped with a one-megaton warhead with from fifty to one hundred times the destructive power of the Hiroshima bomb.

The United States has dropped 180 pounds of bombs for every man, woman and child in both North and South Vietnam.

The United States has dropped 25 tons of bombs for every square mile of territory in both North and South Vietnam.

Is there a law of compensation for the uses of power, Jesus? I wonder how mercy and responsibility should be balanced with self-interest. I ask myself what security really means, Lord. Ultimately it seems to be concerned with living at peace in the world with other people.

Can we achieve that kind of security, Jesus?

A high-school student was talking to me, Jesus.

"I am a stranger to my parents," she said. "They treat me like a child instead of a human being. My mom can't be a friend, only a mother. All my parents do is judge. I don't think they realize how much they have hurt me."

Julie told me that she planned to move away from her family and start life on her own as soon as she reached the age of eighteen.

"I've tried harder than you know to communicate with my mom and dad," she continued. "They don't hear me. They don't understand what I tell them. I don't see why they can't unbend and be human. Lately I've given up trying. I'm just indifferent and don't say anything. I keep out of their way and stay out all the time except when I sleep. It's better this way. There's less friction."

Soon after this conversation I chatted with a parent who is the mother of three children.

"My children are all strangers to me," she said. "Oh, I mean partially, of course. I try to remember what it was like to be a teen-ager, but I can't. So I don't really know what is going on inside their minds. I have a fourteen-year-old girl who is experimenting with marijuana. She didn't tell me. I found out. I must say that I am terrified."

She took a cigarette out of her purse and lit it.

"I consider one of our sons more of a stranger than the others. I wish it were not so. Again, I am not completely serious. But, you see, I don't know where he spends his time. I don't understand his long hair, his politics, or, God help me, what he is doing in his sex life. He deliberately keeps secrets from his father and me. I want to love my three children. I do. They matter more to me than anything else in life except their father. But unfortunately, strangers they remain."

I think that a lot of children and a lot of parents would like to be liberated from being strangers to each other, Jesus. Can they be individuals and still manage to communicate a sense of belonging within a special relationship to each other?

Some parts of virtually everyone's life remain unliberated, don't they, Lord?

So freedom is too often an abstract goal instead of a present reality. How can chains of ignorance and hypocrisy be cast off, Jesus? How can liberation begin inside countless individual bodies and souls, minds and personalities?

It seems that no one is a bystander in the struggle for liberation, Jesus.

She is not yet ten years old, Jesus.

She has been shunted from one rat-infested tenement home to another for as long as she can remember. Her childhood is filled with memories of clogged, dirty toilets, garbage piled up on cracked linoleum floors overrun by roaches, cold winter air hissing through cracks in walls and windows, rainwater pouring down from holes in ceilings, going through days with sucking hunger at the pit of her stomach, the absence of warm clothes, and the growing, gray monotony of beginning to understand what hopelessness is.

She would like to be liberated, Lord.

It sits there in its solitary horror, Lord.

It is a place supposed to house people who are called convicts. That often means poor people, Jesus, who find themselves caught without shining possibilities. When they are caught they have no hopeful way of defending themselves or spelling out to society what a creative second chance might mean.

So they are put here. At different times this place is a snake pit, a torture chamber for the body and mind, a triumphant exhibit of machine and system over men and women, and an obsolete social experiment created by a nation that does not care.

The theory is that if a person is caught, he's guilty, Lord. Cut him off like a dead limb. Turn him into a rotting vegetable. Teach him crimes that he never before dreamed of. Since he's an animal, put him in the jungle. Don't help him to get well, force him to sit it out. Punish, don't cure. Hurt him in a thousand ways, don't let him hold onto a remnant of dignity. Make him pay, don't redeem him. In time society can begin to resemble a rotting vegetable too, Jesus.

Can we tear down this house of horrors, Lord, and start building new lives?

Exploitation disturbs me, Jesus.

It treats all of us as objects. It bothers me most when it is very sincere, easily palatable and disarmingly seductive. So we are sorely tempted, Lord, to buy a product, a personality, a cause, a war, an idea, or even a religion.

Some people end up believing they are exploiting the rest of us for our own good. I wish, Jesus, that all of us would avoid playing God.

He's black and he wants to go to Africa, Lord.

It isn't that he wants to run away. He is trying to find himself. He feels that he cannot do this in a white world with white men, white women, white children, white values, white politics, white religion, white education, white humor, white movies, white television and white leaders.

He is looking for his roots, his past, and his very identity, Jesus. He believes that he would feel free among black people in a black nation.

What is the essence of black and white, Lord? What is their relation to the mystery of our being human?

My God, my God, why hast thou forsaken me?

There is a burst of machine-gun fire and a scream of terror and pain. A hand grenade is hurled into a hut—someone's home—and, moments later, five people are dead and their home destroyed. Someone's crying, Lord. He is being tortured. A woman and her baby are shot down.

My God, my God, why hast thou forsaken me?

The rot and agony of dying are all around us. Sadly, we have passively accepted it for so long that now we can scarcely muster genuine indignation or tears. Death has come to mean an impersonal body count. The word has come to us, night after night, day after day, within the sanctuaries of our homes and over color-TV sets that make the blood look as real as it does in Westerns. But the human blood of young Americans and Vietnamese, Latin Americans and Africans, Arabs and Israelis, is not synthetic. Why—O God—must we tear open human bodies and cause their blood to be shed and drained into the earth?

My God, my God, why hast thou forsaken me?

The Nazi experience: it was only twenty-five years ago. Six million Jews perished in genocide. Organized religion accommodated the state and its own secure position within society. Severe repression lashed out angrily and mercilessly at dissent. The prophets? There were only a few of them. The prophets? Let them be punished—tear out the tongues that offended! Burn the hands that wrote heresy against the state! Lash proud shoulders to wash them in blood! Silence the prophets. Silence them. Silence them.

My God, my God, why hast thou forsaken me?

We shall conquer the moon and space. We shall vanquish foreigners who seek self-determination and move against our wishes or national policy. We shall defend the power of the status quo against the rising aspirations of the young, poor people, black people, Chicanos, native American Indian people. Our future—is it written in plastic, in chrome, in dollars, in monumental waste, in guns, in nuclear overkill, in whiteness that is opposed to color, in respectability that breeds on personal salvation with indifference to the needs of others, in morality that is offended by the act of love but not the act of death?

My God, my God, why hast thou forsaken me?

We mark the death of Christ, the death of the world. We look ahead to the possibility of imprisoning life if we remain deadened to change, accept dumbly what is told us, and bury dissent and therefore democracy.

It is a time of self-examination, looking inward toward the conscience—and therefore out at the world; seeking to identify with the suffering and death of Jesus—as well as that of Christ within our brothers—in order to participate in resurrection.

43

PRAYERS FOR
SEXUAL
HUMANNESS

What can marriage mean, Jesus?

They wonder once again, but now it is a little late to ask. The church is decorated with candles to provide light for their evening wedding.

Their parents are up front. Guests, including lots of school friends, have crowded into the Gothic structure. A former roommate of his is playing guitar music softly. A former roommate of hers will read a poem.

The minister will say ". . . to have and to hold from this day forward, for better for worse, for richer for poorer, in sickness and in health, to love and to cherish, till death us do part . . ."

They feel separate from each other, as they haven't in months. For one thing, they haven't slept together during the past week, since they've both been living in their old homes again. Too, they are anxious about this public proclamation of themselves. They hope it will not bruise something sensitive and private in their love, Lord.

The procession is moving up the aisle, Jesus.

How do loving and liking relate, Lord?

He is forty-five, professionally successful and socially integrated into several groups of interesting people. He likes to have sex with a lot of women, but is desperately afraid of loving them. It is love that he is afraid of. It might open up his life, and then the barriers constructed around his vulnerability could fall down.

So he plays the tough guy with machismo, the laughing man, the big spender and the cynic. When all these roles come together, they lay a heavy weight on a highly insecure, man-sized boy who is afraid to grow up. Not only are women objects to him but he remains an object to himself.

He's telling another story, Jesus. People around him are laughing. He is strutting, building his yarn to its climax—a middle-aged kid with his slingshot.

Can he find that love is childlike instead of childish, Jesus?

"I'm tired of one-night stands," the young woman told me, Jesus.

She has heard all the theories about how smart it would be to wait until she is past thirty before getting married, Jesus, and she doesn't agree.

The young woman is very pretty, with dark, luminous eyes and black hair combed straight back. She works as a secretary in an office.

"Not many guys who take me out want any emotional involvement," she said. "The minute I say that I care, it's split—out the door, out the window. They don't want to get into feelings."

She smiled sadly.

"I want to get married and have kids. But I don't see this happening to me. Not with any of the guys I know. Not if I stay here. Not if I go on living as I've been doing. But what else can I do? It scares me. If I try to change, I know that I'll find out how many things in life now aren't real for me."

How can she handle realities in her life, Jesus? Will she be able to live with feelings and emotions in the open?

He doesn't know if he is afraid of sex or not, Jesus.

He is thirty-five, good-looking, active in public life, and homosexual. He found out, or finally accepted the fact, that he was gay before a brief and sad marriage terminated.

So he went through the gay bars like a house afire. He had a lot of sex with a lot of partners. He learned many tricks, swung with a hip style, accepted his new happiness, and then one day realized that he didn't want raw sex anymore without someone to love.

But this meant an open social acceptance of his homosexuality. He didn't want to define himself that way. Wasn't he human first of all? Yet society would deny that. A whole identity crisis, to be lived in public, confronted him.

He continues looking for the man with whom he can share love, working against the pressures that would confine him to sex without love or life without the kind of fulfilling sex that he seeks.

Can his fears be resolved, Jesus?

How can people free rather than imprison each other in relationship, Lord?

This is the question she asks every time she meets a new man in whom she might be interested.

She got a divorce six months ago. As a matter of fact, she still loves her former husband. She admits that love and hate are close. But she couldn't live with him anymore. Life with him became claustrophobic. She wonders if perhaps she married him too early, before she had more sexual experiences. Anyhow, she saw it through. The kids are grown and in college.

She's free. However, she's lonely in the mornings, the late afternoons and at night. She drinks too much. She isn't sure whom she should sleep with, but she has learned that a lot of sexual advances are made to a divorcee, especially by her former husband's best friends.

She wants a relationship with a man to free her from the prison of her loneliness and self-destruction, Lord. But she wonders if relationship itself ever means freedom.

What is sex, Jesus?

He was taught that it meant the sex act. His instruction took place in the basement of a neighboring house several years ago when some older boys decided to share the facts of life with him. His mother and father never did. His school never did.

Now he is a high-school student. He has begun to realize that sex seems to be a part of breathing, looking, touching, thinking and living. Yet he knows it is also a precise act at a particular time. He has experienced that act with a girl. He has masturbated.

None of this makes him feel at all disturbed except for the fact that a lot of people probably say he shouldn't have done these things. He wonders why.

He expects to be living his life with his sex drive for a long time. He would like to avoid hang-ups. He would rather not hurt anyone else because of sex. He wishes there could be more openness and less hypocrisy about something that seems to be so essential in everybody's life. He has talked with friends recently about the possibility of one day having a vasectomy so that he won't contribute to bringing too many children into the world.

Sex seems nice as well as a somewhat complicated thing to him, Jesus.

She was telling me about her search for love, Lord.

The young woman, a high-school graduate who works in a suburban office, met a man and went to bed with him. He was not the first.

"We bumped into each other, literally, and he kissed me. I was on my coffee break, he was passing through the building. We talked for a while and I agreed to a rendez-vous. I said I didn't want another love thing. He said he was married and had two children.

"I began to see Frank for an hour here and there. About two months later we were in love. Frank was sick about it. He didn't want it any more than I did. I didn't think about anything when I was with him. Just us. We talked so very much. More than we made love, even.

"Through all this I was pregnant with another man's child. That was a one-way, sex-for-love relationship. I had needed love but took sex instead, hoping Ralph might begin to love me if I pleased him. When I told him I was bearing his child he could have killed me. After the things he said I did die partially.

"And that was that. Don't bother him anymore about it. Ever. I wanted my baby so very much. But without a father, without anyone in the world except me, and me without money, she couldn't have had a chance. She was adopted by a young couple.

"My baby was so beautiful. I held her in my arms before I gave her over. She looked at me so angrily. But she'll learn someday how much I had to love her to give her up. Every time I think of her I cry, as I'm doing now.

"Now it's many months since I had her. I had to quit

my job because the strain was so great. I've only spoken to Frank a few times, briefly. We want to see each other often again. Conditions aren't right yet, but they probably will be soon. Regardless of the way I am, I'm me, and that's all there is."

Lord, I couldn't help wondering how long she would try to cover up her loneliness. Can she find the love that she is looking for, Jesus?

What does it mean to create a baby, Lord?

They're married and asking themselves the question. It frightens them, Jesus.

They don't want to program another human life. They don't want to be stuck with authority roles that they have come to question in experiences with their parents. And they are not sure that they will remain married, for they question permanent monogamy and the strength of the family as an institution.

They have thought of becoming part of a commune. A baby would grow up inside a commune with a number of different parental figures. But, it occurs to them, the commune experience might be as temporary as their marriage.

They want to know, Lord, what a baby would really mean in their own lives and as a new human being in life itself.

She used to be too boldly aggressive about sex, Lord.

That is what her family and friends led her to believe. One close friend asked over drinks once if she was a nymphomaniac.

This led her into a long period when she has repressed her feelings. She was ashamed of the passion and joy she experienced in making love. She grew wary of her image as a fun-loving and warm woman. Her husband never seemed to understand her passion, for he wished to place his wife on a kind of pedestal. However, when she denied full expression to her sexual feelings, he proceeded to have an affair with another woman.

The question of how natural one should feel about sex has plagued her ever since. Should someone civilized, particularly a woman, tame or deny natural sexual instincts and instead play a programmed role even in bed with her husband? It is the question she asks. It seems to deeply affect her humanness.

Can she accept sex as a natural part of her life, Jesus, and also find acceptance in that naturalness?

They have been in love for forty years, Lord.

They will be the first to say that it wasn't all a bed of
roses. They accepted their marriage as the most important fact in their lives, so they simply spent more time
and energy on it than on anything else.

Of course, this meant not spending time and energy on
each other beyond a point. Instead they got involved,
often separately, with a lot of other people and their
concerns.

Humor has helped them a lot. The discipline of getting on with it in place of wondering whether they ought
to or not. Listening as well as speaking. A healthy development of sexual fantasy to let sex remain exciting, not
become routine. And unrelenting awareness of how sti-
flingly boring boredom can be.

They give a lot of love to life, Jesus.

PRAYERS
IN THE
SEASONS

I feel a dead leaf on the weathered branch of a black tree, Jesus.

Between my fingers it is like crisp parchment.

The wind blows steadily on this early April afternoon as I walk through a cemetery.

A graying tombstone announces:

JOHN G   1829-1862
His Wife
JUDITH ANN   1835-1909
Daughter
NANCY MARGARET   1859-1937.

An immense brown monument contains a single name, Esher, and a gigantic cross. Two orange flowerpots, one empty, the other half-filled with dirt, are overturned beneath it in the dancing shadow of moving paper leaves.

There, in the distance, a small green pine indicates life. An American flag waves in the wind, over there to the left, in front of a headstone. A wreath of dead flowers with a large, dirty red bow marks a tomb directly in front of me.

I am walking over the dead. Their flesh has vanished. I suppose their bones remain. I do not wish to dishonor them by treading them underfoot. It is the spring earth I seek communion with.

WIFE OF THOMAS PHIPPS
DIED 1893
AGED
48 YRS. 6 MO.
REST IN PEACE.

An angel—How did I know?—this baby figure with immense wings, carved out of stone, is blowing a trumpet
over a grave to my left. A car drives into the cemetery and
moves slowly past me. Two women stop for a moment,
not getting out of the car. They look silently toward a
grave. Then they drive on, around the sloping road and
outside again. The wind is noisy today. A small bird, flying over me through gaunt branches, chirps simple, un-
pretty notes.

I am startled to find that I have almost walked on a
piece of ice (Why hasn't it melted?), the sole remnant
of the winter's last snowstorm a week ago. A fly zooms in
front of me, smelling me before pirouetting away.

MOTHER
ANNE

An urn of artificial flowers appears now on my left. A
sacrificial lamb is carved atop a tombstone bearing the
name Lucia. A wooden, suffering, thorn-crowned Christ
is crucified over a tomstone nearby, surrounded by small
pine trees.

MY-SELF proclaims one small tombstone. The sunlight catches the surface of a distant stone, making it
shine like a windowpane. A six-year-old boy was buried

here; a tiny cement angel bearing a cross recalls him. Ashes to ashes. "A Native of Ireland" says a stone *there*. Dust to dust. Passion lurks in dust. There is a heartbeat in ashes. Who can define ashes? Who can label dust? I walk through the shadow cast by a large white angel, its hands lifted high.

I do not feel sad, Lord. I am peaceful and resting here, catching my breath, alive for a moment amid the death of life outside: car fumes, the drone of television, people rushing to keep pace with machines, racism, war, and encroaching rage. Jesus, this seems to be one of the few quietly reflective places left in the world. Lord, I am grateful to be alive.

It is raining on a summer afternoon, Jesus.

I am looking through a cardboard box of old letters and photographs in the attic. The sound of the falling rain on the wooden roof is gentle, Lord.

Here, handwritten by my grandmother, who died many years ago, is a recipe for jelly roll. 3 eggs. ½ cup sugar. ⅔ cup flour, ¾ tsp. baking powder. Butter a shallow pan. Bake in a quick oven.

Michael's letter before he committed suicide at Oxford. Postcards Jean sent from the Greek Islands the summer she visited there.

The last letter I received from my father before he died. His writing is wobbly, not so firm as it was before his illness. "I love you dearly, son."

The whole world, do you have it in your hands, Lord?

It was autumn, Jesus.

I was in my old house, set back from the road among tall trees. It had been sold, and I would have to depart the next morning so that the new owners could move in.

On that last night I sat late by the hearth. The flames of a roaring fire illuminated the red bricks of the grate and the dull bronze andirons. Sparks flew with abandon up the chimney, and I thought the roof of the house, with its pile of banked dead leaves, would surely catch fire.

It had seemed at first that the great log would not burn. It sputtered mildly. I rolled up more newspaper pages into balls and placed them strategically, with kindling wood underneath and around the log. Finally it caught, crackling with unabashed zest and immense exuberance; but it took hours to burn out.

At the end there were just blazing-hot, ruby-red coals on the floor of the hearth, sending light and heat into the cold—and, I am convinced, haunted—room, making weaving shadows play like friendly ghosts on the ceiling and walls. I sat looking at the fire. An hour passed, then another. I could not persuade myself to go. I would not be able to sit again before this hearth, warming myself and dreaming, communing with the past of this lovely and gracious house.

I slept there before the hearth that night. My emotions were dry and stored away the next morning when I departed. But why did I have to leave? Why do we let life do things to us, Jesus? Aren't we in charge, Lord?

We are the people who rule the earth, they say. Machines exist only to serve us. Life is a mechanism, an experience, under our control. If I was meant to have dominion over animals and machines and time and the exigencies of life, why am I not the ruler? But, Jesus, I am a slave. Is it enslavement to forces inside or outside myself, Lord?

Jesus, I do not want to be the ruler, but I do want to be free.

I am looking through a window, Lord, at snow and ice on the ground outside.

Suddenly a small rabbit darts across my line of vision. It pauses, trembling, beside a frozen bush. Now it runs across an exposed patch of ground, stopping beneath a tree. I can scarcely discern its body in the dark shadows.

The rabbit lives in the grip of death. So do I, Jesus. The purity of air and water concern him as much as me. A nuclear war or accident would destroy us both. His tiny gray body and mine—larger, differently formed—are vulnerable together on the face of the earth, Lord.

If people want to destroy themselves, Jesus, they should take a vote among the animals, the flowers and the trees. Any decision to die should be a democratic one.

The snow is falling, Jesus.

PRAYERS IN A
BLACK STUDENT
CENTER

"How do you see your role?" a black student asks me.

"I don't have a role," I reply. "I'm tired of all roles. I simply want to be myself. I don't want to wear a mask. I only want a face."

There is a ripple of laughter in the Black Student Center, Lord. I realize that it might be easier for me than for anybody else inside that room not to have a role to play. It is easier for me to claim anonymity in my whiteness. I have become the invisible man in a population explosion.

But how does my young black questioner see his role, Jesus?

"The only racists are blacks."

Seated inside the room filled with blacks except for myself, I recollect these words spoken by a white man two weeks earlier, Lord.

The white man had seen headlines and TV reports about black separatism, black rage, black self-determination and black nationalism. No one had explained to him why blacks were acting according to an unfamiliar script.

Wasn't integration the desired goal? I wished that he could hear the words of a black speaker inside the Center who said, "In the integration movement, whites controlled the traffic and selected the vehicles. They were half-stepping in double time."

In other words, Jesus, whites seemed to select a few blacks and then turn them into colored white men and women. It didn't work.

But I realize again, Lord, the wonderful irony of how deeply blacks and whites are brought together by mutually accepted separation in certain areas of life for the sake of liberation as a mutually accepted goal. This is sophisticated instead of simplistic. It demands a lot of honesty on the part of blacks and whites alike.

I become worried, Lord, by the dangers of isolation. Blacks need to understand the subtle changes taking place in that spectrum called "white opinion," as whites need to realize that they are not confronting a black monolith, but individual black people representing a complex of views.

Doesn't racism exist, Jesus, so long as we look at any other human being and see a racial mask instead of a human face?

Black isn't chic anymore, is it, Jesus?

I mean, whites no longer define it as glamorous, "now," or "in." The college men and women in this Black Student Center are on the whole pleased by their drop from fashion, Lord. They want to take care of serious business. Unlike their parents, they have entered into black awareness without an internal struggle. They're interested in getting an education and a solid piece of the action for black people.

Whites are welcomed to the Center if they wish to come. Their embarrassment or uptightness is seen by the black students as important in teaching whites what it has long been like to be black inside a white world with white institutions.

The Center is a remodeled house on the edge of the campus. There is a library of books about the black experience, an office for Afro-American Studies, a social room and a basement hall for lectures or dancing.

Looking at me, the black students' faces are quizzical but not unfriendly. I am received with open courtesy and frank talk. One particularly militant student says that he hopes I will not misconstrue his lack of warm pretense as a sign of belligerence.

What is happening in the Black Student Center gives me hope for all of us, Jesus.

"A White Man's Heaven Is a Black Man's Hell."

I heard this song many, many times when it was sung by young black nationalists in rural Mississippi and Alabama during civil-rights demonstrations in the early sixties. Would these black students, seated in their Center, sing it too?

Yes, I suppose so, Lord. At least they would think it. For their experience of human life has been very hemmed in by white power, hasn't it, Jesus? I imagine they dream of getting away, even just once, from white judgments, ways of doing things, and ingrained attitudes toward black people.

This must be why, Lord, an occasional black professor is such a welcome change from a white one. And a black administrator, a black judge, a black journalist, a black TV personality, a black priest and a black mayor.

A white man's heaven. It would be hell in its isolation, wouldn't it, Jesus?

Would genocide against blacks be possible, Jesus?

I watch black fury on the one hand, and white non-understanding of it, coupled with fear and angry hurt, on the other.

White ignorance about black experience in America now seems almost deliberate, Lord. Nor do whites know the actual conditions (around a corner in the city or across a town) in which blacks live day by day in second-, third- or fourth-class citizenship. I am talking not about the small middle class but about the masses.

Whites and blacks do not know each other in relaxed, honest, open ways. They often meet in time-clock situations, and then the time runs out, the alarm clock goes off.

A black student at the Center mentions the question of genocide. It has a way of being asked. Perhaps the very recent death of six million Jews in Europe automatically demands its consideration.

Such genocide here seems impossible to me, Jesus. But then I remind myself that I am white. I forget the white genocide against Native Americans that happened here. There was the deep burst of feeling against Japanese-Americans in World War II. With its irrational fears and unconfessed sins, that happened here.

As a white, how can I help to make this question an unreal one? If I were black, would I consider genocide in America an impossibility, Lord?

Why do many people simply see violence in black and white, Lord?

I remember when a white student shouted to a black student during a demonstration on a campus: "Come on! We're going to burn the place down!" "No," said the black student. "I want an education. I want one for my brother and sister too."

Don't whites need to understand white consciousness, Jesus, as blacks need to understand black consciousness? In this way, both might come to comprehend human consciousness.

What is black consciousness, Lord? It seems to comprise many things—an understanding of what slavery did to men and women, soul music, Afro hair, African history, soul food, pride in identity, hip, a life style that differs from the white, survival under oppression, blackening the mind, and cool.

What is white consciousness, Lord? It seems to comprise many things—an understanding of what a feeling of superiority instead of equality did to men and women, European tradition, the legacy of puritanism, ethnic background, guilt, ownership of property, creating God in the likeness of a white man, the illusion of a master race, and success, with its nightmare companion, failure.

Tell us about human consciousness, Jesus.

"I don't want to live in a South Africa," a white student told me the other day.

He referred, Jesus, to the separatism between black and white students on his campus. According to him, the blacks eat alone at separate tables in the dining hall, do not always acknowledge a friendly greeting outside a classroom, limit relationships with whites to an absolute minimum of contact, and spend most of their time inside the Black Center.

The white student explained that he didn't feel he should be made to pay for the sins or failures in race relations of his grandparents or parents, Lord.

His comments reminded me of something a black student had said. "I'll refuse from now on to be a textbook for whites. If they want to know about blacks, they should learn it from books or their professors. On my own time, I need to study or be with friends to relax. I'm not going to teach a white kid with my life all the time."

Be with the black student, Lord, and be with the white student, and help each to understand the other's feelings.

I feel so old when it comes to blacks and whites, Jesus.

I mean, I can remember only a few years ago when blacks and whites could not eat together in a public dining room or stay at the same hotel. Looking now at the black students surrounding me, I realize this is a part of their folklore or past history, and does not concern their present experience.

I recollect a visit I paid to a university in the South, Lord, several years ago. Whites and Negroes—as blacks were then called—were scattered through the dining hall at a luncheon in my honor. That is to say, people were not seated in rigid color blocs. This seemed healthy and promising. But I was wrong, Jesus.

Most of the whites and blacks present had never laid eyes on each other before. Blacks were singularly unwelcome here. The atmosphere could have been cut with a very sharp knife. Nobody seemed to breathe normally.

When this reality finally got through to me, I tried to break the tension. I told a few of the extremely funny, warm and earthy stories that had grown out of the civil-rights struggle, these seeming to represent about the only really spontaneous and present American humor still in existence. No one laughed, Jesus.

Zeroing in, I told facts about second-class citizenship and the truth about the black experience in white America. I thought it was time these people heard about such things, especially as they were seated in an integrated group that apparently would not soon, if ever, be duplicated. Again, breathing had stopped.

Inside that room, Lord, both the blacks and whites had

been conditioned—for how long?—not to trust each other at all. They had been taught not to look at each other as human beings but only as "Negroes" and "whites." Later I was told that most whites seated in that room had been taught by their churches, newspapers, schools and families that civil-rights activists, and others involved in the racial struggle for justice, were indisputably members of the Communist party.

Many people have died for the cause of human liberation, Lord. Will it be won?

Black is not alien to me, Jesus.

It used to be. It was different, so I feared it. White was supposed to be clean, pure and holy. Black, I learned, was its opposite. Wasn't black a coal pit of sin and a moonless night of death?

I saw a black face, Lord. It smiled at me. Then I saw the Manichaean contrast of white teeth. I could not smile back. Who was this strange creature who greeted me? What harm did he mean to do to me? I had to ask myself, Lord, if he was human.

The first time I was alone as a white in a room filled with black men and women I was disturbed, Jesus. I tried to breathe evenly. What was expected of me? I laughed, smiled, frowned, told jokes, and sought emotional refuge.

Now I can discern black friendship, black anger, black hurt, black love, black deceit, black rage and black tenderness. These are human, Lord, and a part of me.

Black is not alien to me, Jesus.

PEOPLE

It was a swinging party, Jesus.

But the people seemed to be tense. They were in constant motion and playing tight roles. Everybody was scripted and choreographed. Booze covered up a multitude of neuroses. Celebration! Everybody was to have fun!

I saw a woman dressed in gold pajamas and enough costume jewelry to sink an excursion boat. She had had too much to drink. She kept saying, "I want to work with the poor in Africa. . . . The poor . . . Africa . . . I want to work with the poor in Africa."

I wondered what she really wanted, Lord, and what was her Africa.

A heavy frame separates me from the bearded man in the painting, Jesus.

Does it provide him with an illusion of noninvolvement?

He is yawning. Now he begins coming through to me as someone trying to play a smug role. He is not succeeding, for I see through his painted outer mask of charming dilettantism and exaggerated ease.

The man painted in oils inside the frame that separates us is not relaxed at all, Lord. Neither am I. We need to talk.

I would like to throw away all frames.

**He doesn't know how his children are going to eat to-
night, Jesus.**

There is just no money left. He has tried everything
but cannot find a job. His wife is sick and doesn't have
the right kind of care.

His little girl is crying. The sound of it is a bit louder
than the dialogue of an old movie that is playing on the
TV set. His boys are sitting huddled on an old sofa,
watching the images flicker on the television screen.

Lord, he wishes that he knew what to do.

She is outwardly a very, very correct woman, Jesus.

But her interior life is in disarray. She suspects that she may be having a long and continuous nervous breakdown.

It isn't that she can't function, Lord. She goes through all the motions excellently. However, she hasn't even the vaguest idea of what she truly believes about anything. Her identity is a remote face that she looks at in the mirror of a morning, adding a touch of rouge here, a bit of powder there, and now contemplating a pleasant smile, perfect white teeth, and a hint of mystery within the eyes.

She is searching for a handy kind of magic glue, Lord, to hold together lots of broken pieces that comprise what is known as her life: car keys, office-door keys, desk keys, apartment keys, a social security number, pills, photographs, telephone numbers, credit cards, a jigger of fear, a dash of loneliness, and she has to hurry now.

Can she connect the outside of her life with the inside of it, Jesus?

She is in high school, Jesus.

While she was growing up, social issues held the center
of the stages of her life. There was talk about freedom,
which many different people felt they had been denied.
This made her wonder about her own freedom, Lord.

"I've become free all around," she said, her face breaking into a happy grin.

"Through the teaching of freedom by close friends and
Gibran and Gandhi and Diogenes and others, I realized
my freedom through the words of my sociology teacher
in our high school. A surprise package came with my
freedom, if being freer weren't enough, but I am more
and more becoming and *being* nonviolent. This is a very
important thing to me."

Her eyes search the ground and the sky outside the big
window alongside us.

"You know what I've discovered—realized—through
others' realizations? That I am unable to love. To love
one single person in a romantic boy-girl relationship.
That people, my age especially, think love is a cow when
it's really an elephant. They're always believing an elephant is a cow—and no wonder there are so many divorces
when people marry merely for love.

"So now that I realize that I can't love and won't be
able to love for quite a while—well, no sweat. I can be
freer. All of which does not mean that I can act and react lovingly. And when I *know* that I don't know what
love is, I can't be hurt by it. Lord, I'm a kite!"

Help her to share her freedom, Jesus.

Everywhere I see color, Lord.

A brown man wearing a red shirt, blue coat, checkered vest and striped pants is walking across a yellow bridge in the park. Surrounding trees are green. Beneath the bridge the water is silver. The sky is trumpet-blue.

Where is the man in the colored world going, Jesus?

Today she is seventy years old, Lord.

Everybody else is concerned about her birthday celebration while she is cooking breakfast and planning a visit to the grocery store.

It doesn't seem possible to her that she is seventy. Where did the years go? Her interests and thoughts are very young ones, moving backward swiftly over many years.

Where did the last week go so quickly? The last day—the last hour? Time is running through a sieve.

But, of course, she is not bound by it. She is free. Fear is merely a word. She sees her mother and father. Remember the picnic when she turned ten years old? She sees her college roommate and her Latin teacher and her husband and her baby and . . .

Somebody is telephoning to wish her a happy birthday.

She doesn't understand why nobody seems to realize how young she really is, Jesus.

Two Seminarians: A Dialogue-Prayer for the Church

JOHN:

I'm packed.

    I'll be ready to go after chapel and breakfast in the
        morning.

    It will be strange not to be here.

    I'm a stranger to the man I was.

Bill and I entered the seminary together.

    We were giving our lives to the church.

    What were we like three years ago?

    Bill has changed as much as I have.

    He's staying here.

    It isn't simply staying or leaving that is important, but
        what's honest for a man to do.

My life has never been so right as it is now.

    There's the feeling of a clean line about it.

    Tomorrow. Tomorrow morning I'll leave.

BILL:

My world, it's been shaken to its foundations.

    John didn't know what conflict he started in my life
        when he decided to leave.

    At first I thought I should go with him.

I've been critical of the same things.

    I've felt the same futility and hopelessness.

    Nothing *really* seems to change.

    This, despite changes.

    But afterward you look closely and see no changes.

The reason I'm not going with John is that I still think
there is hope working for change in the church from
the inside.
I believe in the foundations and essential structure of
the church.
In the long run, John may do more by leaving the seminary to preserve the essential structure of the church
than I'll do by staying.
Only time will tell.

JOHN:

I feel that I finally know who I am.
It isn't easy for me to leave the seminary.
I've put my whole life into this.
Future directions are hazy for me. There's no easy
road map to follow.
The alternatives are potentially cruel, but I'm no longer
so afraid of cruelty.
I'm more afraid of dishonesty, especially in myself.
It's honest for Bill to stay.
It's honest for me to go.
If I have to suffer some hardships now, I say yes to it.
I acknowledge my needs as a man.
I can't think only about tomorrow.
I must be a whole man today.

BILL:

Yesterday. Today. Tomorrow.
How do these relate?

I respect the traditions of yesterday.
I want to live fully today.
I believe in the fulfillment of tomorrow.
Does this make me a conservative?
John places today ahead of yesterday and tomorrow.
Is John a radical?
I think I can be a whole man working inside the system.
It just doesn't threaten my existence.
John forced me to make a free choice.
Stay or leave. Like that.
I'll stay.

JOHN:

After my first year in the seminary, I discovered that I
    knew *everything* about God.
He was omnipotent.
He was omnipresent.
He was omniscient.
He was *He*.
Onward, Christian Soldiers.

BILL:

They taught me never to be angry or lose my temper.
    To love everybody, being available to all people at all
        times.
    To be Christlike.
    To pray more than other people.
Some of my teachers said the church was not involved in
        the sinful world, such as
    real estate

        ward politics
        racism
        war
No.
        It was holy.

JOHN:

A clergyman will
        conduct public worship.
        minister to the sick and dying.
        baptize babies.
        marry men and women.
        bury people.
Will a clergyman
        march on a picket line?
        preach a disturbingly honest sermon?
        knowingly lose money for the church by telling the
            truth?
        protest actively against institutional racism?
        stand publicly against war and warfare?
        go to jail for his religious convictions?
        feel lonely?
        fight inside the system to change the system?

BILL:

It was during our first year in the seminary.
        John and I both felt totally inadequate to be here.
        We felt sinful because we didn't love God enough.
        We wanted the drives within us for education and a
            better world to become more holy.

        95

John and I decided to pray together.
  On two nights a week we set our alarm clocks for 2 A.M.
  We met in the chapel.
  We knelt down on the stone floor.
  We prayed silently.
Once we prostrated our bodies, in the form of Christ
    hanging on the cross, on the stone floor of the
    chapel.
  Body of Christ, save us.
  Blood of Christ, inebriate us.
  Passion of Christ, strengthen us.

JOHN:

For an examination, we had to be able to list all the books
    of the Old Testament in order.
  I stayed up all night, cramming.
  Genesis, Exodus, Leviticus,
  Numbers, Deuteronomy, Joshua,
  Judges, Ruth, I Samuel . . .
Study the prophets.
  But don't recognize one sitting in the room with you.
  He might rock the boat.
  He might upset the status quo.
  Study church history but don't make it.

BILL:

The difference a few men made.
  The right time and the right place.
  John XXIII.

He changed the church.
He destroyed the Catholic world.
He destroyed the Protestant world.
Bonhoeffer.
He forced me out of the religious ghetto into the whole
world.
Religionless Christianity.
I'm glad I am living now.
I can stay in the system.
I can help change the system.

JOHN:

The French worker-priests.
They wanted to be close to people.
They didn't want any separation between their lives
and the real lives of ordinary people.
They wanted the church to stand with the poor, not
the privileged against the poor.
The establishment tried to break them.
It failed, although the movement seemed to die or go
underground when it was outlawed.
*Unless a grain of wheat falls into the earth and dies, it
remains alone; but if it dies, it bears much fruit.*
I feel a close kinship to these worker-priests.
My interpretation of them is one reason I'm leaving.
I want to work as a Christian with people's secular
concerns.
I don't want to spend my life and energy battling the
establishment.
Can I bypass it and be a Christian in the world?

BILL:

Why was I born into *this* age?
    Nothing can be the same as it was.
    Old forms don't give new meaning to this generation.
I love old forms.
    To worship before an ancient altar.
    To wear bright vestments.
    To hear the Eucharist sung very, very well.
    I love these things.
    I find them exhilarating and meaningful.
This doesn't mean God is only *here*.
    It means, at its best, that God is here and therefore
        everywhere in his world.
    But this is an age of pragmatism.
    Mysticism must, it seems, be found in involvement in
        the world.
I shall stay in the church and try to build bridges to the
    world outside it.
    John and I will have such a bridge.

JOHN:

For I was hungry and you gave me no food.
I was thirsty and you gave me no drink.
I was a stranger and you did not welcome me.
Naked and you did not clothe me.
Sick and in prison and you did not visit me.
    I'll try to be with Jesus in the world.
    I'll end up working with people, without a collar or a
        portfolio.

Without the church's ordination.
I say yes to this.
As Jesus is in me, I'll be a priest of his.
Social action instead of organized religious activity.
Prayer actions in the place of mere prayer words.
Lord of life instead of Lord of the church.
Liturgy as action in life, not actions in ritual.
I am whole.
I want to be a man for God, in the midst of life.

BILL:

I am whole.
I'll be a juggler, like John.
Like John, I'll try to be a fool for Christ's sake.
There will never again be a neat, ordered pattern for
me.
I can only try to follow Jesus' way of life.
I'll try to do this within the church and the world.
To see through the stained-glass windows.
To see Jesus in people's lives.
To see Jesus resurrected from religious forms as well as
death.
To understand resurrection as freedom.
Not license.
Freedom.
I'll be busy.
John, my brother, what *is* priesthood?
We can try to find out and share it.

PRAYERS ON
CURIOUS
OCCASIONS

I had to say goodbye, Jesus.

The entire incident could now no longer be saved from tears, the whip of fleeting final moments upon tenderness, and the absolute and perhaps merciful blurring of reality.

Then it was done. Goodbye had been said. A door closed. A motor started and disappeared into the distance. My heart that had cracked loudly into many pieces now stopped beating altogether.

Jesus, please share my aloneness. Here, I give it to you, Lord. Please take it, Christ.

It was May Day at a country fair, Jesus.

I found myself in the midst of a slow-moving crowd of people, families with small children carried on their fathers' shoulders, boys and girls barefoot, and elderly people carrying paper bags filled with fresh turnips, onions and squash.

White Baby's Breath was for sale at Stall No. 24. I saw a hand-lettered sign directly in front of me bearing the words *Bleeding Heart. Blooms All Summer*.

A young friend of mine, a six-year-old boy, found hundreds of polliwogs in a water-filled ditch just outside the fair grounds and scooped up one of them in a paper cup. Then, his conscience bothering him, he returned the polliwog to approximately the same spot in the ditch from which it had been taken.

First Ayd said one of the signs outside the Renaissance Pleasure Faire. We were inside the fair grounds now. Four madrigal singers were entertaining a dozen attentive people. Nearly everybody was attired in medieval costume. I had retrieved a bright blue fourteenth-century French chasuble from a trunk where I had long ago packed it away. I wore it, with a matching stole, over an open-necked plain shirt and Levi's. Men and women danced on the green, and hawkers were selling clay flutes. Dogs of all sizes and descriptions were everywhere underfoot. People on horseback rode through the crowd. Signs pointed out *Glassmakers Lane, Potter's Market, Printmakers Way* and *Candlemakers' Cove*. Mead and ale, Cornish pasties, meat pies, popovers, tarts and fyne roasted chycken were available at stalls.

Cameos of Renaissance Drama Including "The Taming of the Shrew" led off the day's bill at the theater. Musical interludes were provided by an Italian Renaissance consort of ancient instruments.

"It's organic—it grows," someone said. "We've tried to reproduce what would actually be at a Renaissance fair. So we have included the Viking heritage, North Africa and, for example, spices that traders in Europe would have brought back from the Orient. The Renaissance fair was a comprehensive world, like the court of that time. One found mixed stations, different back grounds, as people simply mingled together. Villages were too small to have anything but inns, and markets could be found only at the fairs."

I chatted with several new friends. One said that a witch had cast a fertility spell over his house. His wife was pregnant. All the flowers were blooming. Even the cat was having kittens.

A black goat wearing a straw hat ambled by. A tumbling act had concluded, a belly dancer was about to begin. Then she would be followed by a folk singer offering sixteenth-century songs. A sign announced a stall's name, *Earth Mother*. Someone asked me for help. "I'm looking for the Golden Toad, who is the next performer on the stage," she said.

I talked with a student. "Everybody at the fair just gets together and falls into the same mood," he told me. "There's a comfort in being with people you don't know who share the same attitudes and feelings as you do. And it's great to have that happen out in the country on a nice day. The clothes people wear, the colors, the excitement—all this is great. People put on these costumes and become all the exciting people they've always wanted to be. Everybody can do it. There aren't any limits. People can wear flowers in their hair if they want to. People don't have to wear flowers in their hair if they don't want to. It's beautiful."

I burned my mouth eating a hot fruit tart. I drank ginger beer. Someone in the distance was flying a kite. People milled around or sat on bundles of hay observing others. Flags and banners of yellow, orange, blue and red were matched by the colors in people's clothing. A pretty girl offered me a bite of French bread and cheese. The rolling hills and green slopes eased gently down to streams of water where kids were wading. The old trees seemed to be out of Sherwood Forest.

"You walk down most city streets in a costume and you frighten people," someone was saying. "It's sad that people are so jumpy and scared. Here it's a comfortable atmosphere."

Jesus, we need more country fairs, don't we?

Tension had been building to a showdown in our group, Jesus.

I knew my raw nerves were exposed. I had a sudden, vivid awareness that my reserve of patience and energy was all used up. Apparently the others felt the same way.

Everything blew up, Lord. We sat there afterward in silence amid the awful shambles of what we had done to each other. We were frightened and ashamed of being psychically stark naked in front of each other.

There were no recriminations or ritualistic acts of self-justification. But we dug at roots and new beginnings. Feelers were extended gently. Ideas were unraveled. Suddenly it became evident that the incident of violence would hold no explicit reference for us beyond itself.

Most unexpectedly, we all shared a healing experience. Healing can be a funny thing, can't it, Lord?

Mike, my dog, was dying on that rainy day.

"Man" and "Dog." I had often wondered about the relationship between Mike and the human world. How had he looked at life, houses, shops from a speeding car, lights in tall buildings at night, authority and freedom, the human schedule he had grown accustomed to, squirrels and cats—and me?

Mike, who was sixteen years old, somehow got to his feet and stood beside me. I reached out to touch the head and body of a close companion before he died.

How can I understand the mystery of the relationship between animals and humans, Lord?

I have a fever, Jesus.

It paralyzes my senses. I don't have the will or strength to get out of bed. I can scarcely turn my body over. All I seem to want right now is oblivion.

The fever is like an electric current moving behind my eyes and in my limbs. I need to feel cool. Just lying here in bed, scarcely breathing, without making any physical exertion at all, is the closest I can come to feeling cool. I have a capacity for sleep like a blotter for ink.

I took health for granted, didn't I, Lord? Please be master of the fever, Jesus.

It was a curious happening, Jesus.

In the eyes of a tired businessman who watched a long column of college men and women march in front of his car on a downtown city street, the event probably seemed to be an angry, maybe dangerous, student demonstration. Yet, in contrast with such imagery, the occasion was poignant for the youths' helplessness and the gentleness of their sober intensity in the face of a moral outrage.

An hour earlier the plaza on the campus was cold beneath the wind that had a late-winter ferocity. A number of us stood around a makeshift platform. Guerrilla theater players attired in military dress, juxtaposed against policemen in attendance, established a bizarre illusion of a police state.

A mock coffin, draped in black crepe paper, lay on the platform. It bore the name of Pvt. Richard Bunch. Two students, a man and a woman, stood on the platform holding a large banner that read *Free the Presidio* 27. The crowd was composed almost entirely of students, with only a sprinkling of faculty members.

Pvt. Richard Bunch had been shotgunned to death by a guard at the Presidio Military Prison in San Francisco, it was explained to us by a graduate student. He told how twenty-seven other prisoners, protesting the killing of Bunch as well as their own dehumanizing conditions inside the stockade, had been charged with mutiny and confronted with a court-martial.

Standing on the platform inside the campus plaza, the graduate student who was talking loomed above us. He spoke with edgy intensity, letting his utterances fall into a pattern of rat-tat-tat words followed by abrupt, long pauses. He was followed by a young man who had served sixteen and a half months in military prison for refusing to carry a weapon or wear a uniform. His presentation was low-key, though his content was emotionally charged when he asked the spectators to identify themselves with the Presidio guards instead of the prisoners.

Now there was a bit of outdoor guerrilla theater, the military men attacking a victim (Pvt. Richard Bunch). The crowd commenced Pvt. Bunch's funeral procession, which would lead through the streets of the town adjoining the campus to the Selective Service headquarters. I found myself behind several students who wore chains made out of black crepe paper.

One, two, three, four . . . Crunch, crunch, crunch, as our feet marched on the snow, Lord. A red traffic light at the corner, cars waiting, horns blowing. The procession was on its way. Local police provided color, rendering the event excitingly newsworthy for TV cameramen. "Why don't you get a bath and jobs?" shouted a businessman at the students in the procession. The long, winding column passed a downtown store window that held an immense flag-draped color photograph of Richard Nixon.

Women working in the Selective Service headquarters smiled and returned the "V" signs students were making with their fingers. The weather was colder now, as the wind increased in velocity. "Don't leave it on the sidewalk," a policeman told a group of students who were placing the mock coffin of Pvt. Richard Bunch in front of the entrance to the Selective Service headquarters. The students picked up the coffin, placed it on their shoulders, and resumed a clocklike marching procession up one side of the street, down the other, and back again. "Will you please cross at the corner?" asked a cop.

The agony of political helplessness was reflected in many drawn and somber faces of the college men and women. But why didn't more of the people in the town share the students' concern about justice, Jesus?

It is Christmas Eve, Lord.

Outside my window the afternoon light is fading. I'll sit here in the quiet for a few moments before I light the Christmas tree and turn on a lamp.

Other Christmas Eves crowd into my mind, and there is no room. How can I understand Christmas Eve, Jesus, underneath all the tinsel and loud music, the wrapping of presents, and pictures everywhere of you as a baby in a manger?

These next few hours, Lord—will I simply feel emptiness and longing? Will I try to cover them up with laughter and bright light? But I want to feel the deep meaning of this night.

Now it is growing darker outside, Jesus—in a moment I shall turn on the lights. Tell me, Lord, what was Christmas Eve like?

JESUS
PRAYERS

I need to pray again, Jesus.

I grew tired of saying words that I couldn't seem to do anything about. It seemed hypocritical, Lord, to pray when I felt hopeless and sad. I didn't want to go on keeping you at a great distance, asking you to give me just what I thought that I wanted, as if you were magic.

Can't I simply let you be here with me and not ask you for anything? I just want to talk with you and be silent with you. Can't I love you and not use you, Jesus?

Who are you, Jesus?

Many pictures that I see portray you as a white man with blond hair and blue eyes.

A lot of people assume that you were celibate, yet the question has been raised as to whether or not you were married.

Some of us shut out every picture of your life except that of your activism. So you end up basically having an image of becoming angry inside the temple when you overturned the tables of the money changers.

Others of us see you only as quiet and contemplative, a walking example of the Twenty-third Psalm.

I would like to separate fantasy from reality in your life, Jesus.

Do you need me to act as your public-relations man, Jesus?

I don't think you do. I may work in your service, but your success doesn't depend upon my success. You do not fail if I am not effective. This frees me from a terrible slavery to myself under the guise of succeeding for you.

You are not mocked, Lord. Your kingdom has already come. It is established in human life. I can cooperate with it but can never usher it in.

Why do some people say it is necessary to win money, large numbers of converts, publicity and prestige for you? I believe this is a tragic snare and delusion, Lord. It has led to the church's fatal silence on issues where following you would have meant its own loss of these things.

Some Christians speak of the church as an army, Lord. You are presumably the general, and the army is supposed to fight valiantly for your victory in the world, even if it must sometimes kill, maim or pillage.

Is anyone, anywhere, ever meant to be manipulated, sacrificed or dehumanized for your success, Jesus?

A hard question for me is slowly taking formation, Jesus.

Does participation in Christianity mean that a person enjoys the understanding of other people? Or does it imply estrangement, rejection and misunderstanding?

I wonder if perhaps these are the last days of our particular civilization and even the world as man has known it. So can Christianity any longer be the easy, comfortable thing it has seemed in the past for those who never suffered because of their faith? It has become acceptable to make religion a quiet sanctuary in which the cries of the world's pain cannot be heard.

It seems to me that being a Christian now will increasingly involve your cross and many individual crosses, Lord. Maybe Christians will find they can act only out of a sense of conscience and never as participants in a popularity contest.

I ask myself if Christianity will become Christlike. Does anything else about it really matter, Jesus?

You were an anti-hero of your own day, Jesus.

This seems important, because many people tell oppressed victims of society that they should accept things
as they are. You are quoted, Jesus, as saying that some
things belong to Caesar, or his duly constituted overseers,
and other things belong to God.

But is there holy or human justification for unchanged
order under establishment law, Jesus? It is claimed that
you stand for reconciliation. I can understand this and
agree with it. But reconciliation so often becomes sub-
servience to the existing and unjust order instead of justice and change.

The victim of society's cruelty is supposed to be reconciled to his unchanged condition. Why isn't society supposed to be reconciled to the shattering of a false peace
based on injustice, Lord?

Tell me about the Kingdom of God, Jesus.

In terms of my words and concepts, is it conservative, liberal, radical, revolutionary, left-wing, right-wing, none of these, a combination of them, or something altogether different?

I become confused, Lord, when some people claim their way is the sole way of knowing the kingdom. But aren't all of us imperfect in our motives and actions? That is, we tend to be ruthless in order to achieve change and satisfied with the status quo, satisfied with our methods for change and ruthless in preserving the status quo.

Is the Kingdom of God changing all of the time, Lord, or does it remain stable? In the Kingdom of God, what does "revolutionary" mean?

Do you want me to imitate you, Jesus?

I'm not at all sure that you do. I feel that you probably want me to become fully myself.

But if I wanted to imitate you, Jesus, how could I do it? You were raised in the Jewish religious tradition of your time, I in the Christian religious tradition of my time and place. You lived in a rural, primitive society, while I live in an urban and sophisticated one. You dwelt under Roman occupation, while I live in the Rome of to day as a full citizen. You died on the cross, but today there are only gas chambers, electric chairs and hangmen's nooses. You lived in a world of limited communication between people, while I am surrounded by television, jet planes and teletypes.

But I realize that imitating you, Jesus, doesn't have very much to do with such things as these. It really means imitating your love, your honesty and your commitment, doesn't it?

Even when the church seems remote and cold, I feel that you are very close to me, Jesus. You are not a distant savior. You are here with me, transforming emptiness into fullness, nothingness into meaning, impersonality into identity.

I want to imitate you, Jesus. Help me.

Many of your words seem to be absurd, Jesus.

I mean, they are by the standards of society. You said that the meek will inherit the earth. Men who are reviled and persecuted for your sake are blessed. The kingdom belongs to the poor.

I am reminded of the Theater of the Absurd, Lord, and its use of paradox, poetry and myth to speak about life. It occurs to me that our ways of speaking about the truths of Christianity should be the same. Instead they are sometimes literal, fundamentalistic and dogmatic. Perhaps Christianity ought to be called the Faith of the Absurd.

It is certainly contrary to reason, Lord, to exalt valleys, say that the first shall be last and the last shall be first, turn water into wine, raise Lazarus from his tomb, announce that the Kingdom of God is in the midst of human life, die between two thieves on a garbage heap, and refuse to remain dead.

Isn't the absurdity of holiness the closest thing to its essential truth and purity, Jesus?

I want to be with you, Jesus, and I don't want to be.

Sometimes I feel that if you would just go away and leave me alone, I could make it. I mean, I could strike a neat balance between involvement and personal security. I could have some things my way, you could have some things your way, and I would very religiously and faithfully make the decision.

There are moments when I must ask myself the question, What do you want of me, Lord? I am generally a decent sort, basically loving, outgoing, respectable, hardworking, unself-righteous, generous and steady.

Do you want my heart, Lord? Do you want my mind, Lord? Do you want my soul, Lord?

I find it very hard to give them to you. Please don't quit fighting me, Jesus.

PRAYERS IN
STRUGGLE

Don't crush me.

The walls are shifting slowly, easing toward me; they are liquid yet still contain form, like a wave. Only they move very, very slowly; smoothly and imperceptibly, Jesus. I must not cease my vigil for even a moment. The walls might crush me in a sudden, violent, single action.

Otherwise nothing seems to be happening, Lord. A deceptive calm has filled the room if not my life. A still life on the wall breathes gently. The patterns of a rug clash silently. A great colorful poster looks down, lifeless; how can it possess color if not life?

Ideas, like a rising wind, stir dangerously in my mind.

The walls have shifted again, rhythmically. Now they have come closer, Jesus. I rise to my feet, my powers tensed, and confront the walls. "Stand back!" I shout at the walls and whatever lies behind them. "Stand back!"

Isn't activism without involvement a delusion, Jesus?

I mean, wheels can be spinning. Ego needs can be met by ceaseless work. Guilt can be assuaged by self-righteousness. Everything can be organized on a big basis down to the least detail. But what if there is no involvement of feeling, Lord?

It worries me when activism is very romantic. Doesn't it become a form of escapism? Active people then seem to be locked inside smiling iron masks, performing good works on an automated assembly line. But it is antiseptic charity, Lord. People don't touch.

Don't good works have to get mixed up with blood, sweat and tears, Jesus?

I sit inside my jail, Jesus.

I constructed it with my own hands, stone upon stone, lock inside lock. Here I am a model prisoner of my own will. Here I am the slave of self.

Freedom is what I long for, Lord. My weary body and tired mind cry out for new life. My soul is parched and life is in decay, with dreams crumbled and energy stifled. Depression is heavy upon me. I feel hopeless in this moment, Jesus. I am only sorry for myself. I ask if there is any use to struggle with life.

But still I want a voice to cut through my silence, Jesus. Let me hear laughter. Let me see a burst of light.

I want to care again, Lord.

How machinelike can humans become, Lord?

It was a hot day. Driving down a hill, I could see the backs of a dozen or more cars ahead. Their rear lights would flash on—red! click!—then a few feet farther they would turn off. Now on again—red! click!—off. On. Off. On. Off. On Off. Fifty times going down the winding hill road.

My lights were doing the same thing, Jesus, as I placed my foot on the brake and took it off. On. Off. Was I operating the machine or was it really operating me? Everybody else looked funny, I thought, sitting inside the plain or brightly colored machines they were driving.

A lot of machines and people seemed to look alike. I mean, the appearances of the people seemed to fit the personalities of the cars they had selected. Did I look like my car? I may even have behaved like it. A question formed in my mind, Lord. Why do machines sometimes behave like the worst humans, and humans like the worst machines?

I have tried not to live an insular life, Jesus.

But it has been hard. A white, middle-class American is so marked in the world. He is a Roman with his power and money. I mean, I have never known what it really feels like to be Spanish or Turkish or Brazilian.

Of course, I have never known how it feels to be black. I have wanted to get inside a black skin, crawl behind a black face and look out through those eyes at myself. I never could. I could only look through my own eyes at black skin, Afro hair, and growing rage.

Which are faces, Jesus, and which are masks? Identities are so often mysteries. There are moments, Lord, when I wonder if I have ever known how it feels to be myself.

I wish that I knew what to do with memories, Lord.

Some things that I remember are too painful for me to bear. I try to hide them underneath layers of other thoughts. I try to keep busy so that I won't have time to think about them.

But at an unexpected moment in the middle of the day the memories and I are alone. They are remembrances of people I loved who are no longer here with me. They are thoughts about what might have been, Jesus. I wish that I had acted differently about many things. I can see how I took the wrong turning in this road and that path. Why didn't I understand how a blow to my pride was justified, Lord? I couldn't seem to see my life in an intelligent perspective and make the right choices.

What can I do with my life, Jesus, so that I can live in peace with memories?

He seemed to be a close friend, Lord.

Now I feel that he is a distant stranger. We are not communicating with each other at all.

Was I wrong before, Jesus? Am I wrong now?

It had always seemed to me that he and I looked at things in the same way. I felt that he knew my thoughts and ideas without my having to spell them out. I believed that I knew his.

Suddenly my friend's face became an alien mask. His ideas disturbed me. I could not share them at all. He expected me to do something that I could not do if I were to remain myself.

So a gulf has come between us, Lord. We are no longer friends. If we avoid contact, can we stop short of becoming enemies?

It makes me wonder what friendship really means, Jesus. Can my friend and I bridge the gulf that has grown between us? How can we do it, Lord?

I believe that terror is evil, Jesus.

Sometimes I am tempted to use it when I angrily protest against the terrorism of the status quo. An eye for an eye. A tooth for a tooth. Injustice for injustice. A life for a life.

But if one became a Nazi to defeat Nazism, wasn't he already defeated, Lord? I mean, he had become his enemy. He had allowed his enemy to win.

Murder doesn't win people's hearts. Burning, exploding and destroying don't make people love. "Love" is a misused word, isn't it, Jesus? Some people think it is soft to love. I don't think so. I believe that love can overcome hate. I believe that it can overcome terrorism. But why haven't we ever tried it?

How can I change anything, Lord?

Sometimes I wonder if many people hate too much for there to be any peace or creative change. How much time is left for humans to learn how to love?

A drug addict who said he was a philosopher told me to flee, Lord. He said terrorism is coming. He felt that idealistic people who had exposed their views had to stay out of sight and hidden inside the forests or else had to leave the country.

I am told by some young friends living in communes that a new Dark Age is coming. And that the only way to preserve human values is to nurture them in cocoon-like small communities until the evil has passed. Are they right when they say Armageddon is coming, Lord?

I ask myself if the best way to bring about change is to stay in the heat of battle, with the risk of heightening violence and the possibility of holocaust, or withdraw in silent witness. Should people strike out for survival instead of leading an open, risky life, Jesus?

Time is raging inside me, Jesus.

It is draining me of life. Each second is cruelly racing away from me. An hour seems a monstrous thing beyond my imagination, Lord.

I mean, will life itself be safe? There are so many dangers that threaten it. It seems the ultimate barbarism to destroy it. But the very threat makes it an indescribably rare gift. I cannot take it for granted, Jesus, or waste my life as if it were part of an unlimited supply.

I become frightened. How can I stop this flood of time? I want to shore up the moments.

But please do not calm my desperation. Do not provide any release from my aching fear. For I want to feel alive, commune with nature, and behold wonder through my eyes. I want to touch warm flesh, sense the depth of mystery, and ache with love. I want to perceive what is glowing radiance, outpoured kindness, and the rhythm of delight.

Teach me what life really means, Lord, and how not to waste it.

II

Notes on the Humanistic Revolution:

**A RESTATEMENT
OF THEMES
IN THE PRAYERS**

M<small>ANY</small> people believe that the conditions of *Brave New World*, with their bureaucratic authoritarianism and restrictions on individual freedom, are just around the corner of our human experience. 1984 is not far away. Eugene Ionesco, the Theater of the Absurd playwright who authored *Rhinoceros*, said recently: "My most terrifying image of the future is a universe peopled with wild sheep. And I think we're on our way there."

Is such a doom inevitable? Charles A. Reich, in *The Greening of America*, says it is not. Much of what Reich wrote about "the energy of enthusiasm, of hope" is true, yet his view of the new consciousness is a dangerously romantic and unrealistic one. He seems unfamiliar with the theology underlying such a work as *Lord of the Flies*. He pietistically beholds pure happiness where there is brokenness of spirit and existential agony. He seems to be curiously shut off from the suffering and rage of dispossessed people. He remains naïvely unaware of the extent to which "cultural revolution" has shrewdly been co-opted by political and commercial traffickers in human flesh and spirit. His view of life, in fact, appears to lack an awareness of the tragic dimension.

Peter Marin wrote in a prophetic and highly critical comment about Reich's work in *The New York Times Book Review*: "My bones and the lives of my friends tell me that we are already two steps into an ice age, a dark age of the soul, what my friends call 'the long march'—a long, bitter struggle for psychic survival." He went on to state:

Reich's thesis is perhaps half-right: there *is* an opening up, a new sense of space. But that space is also a void, a terrifying sense in the young of disconnection, impotence, sorrow and rage that exceeds anything one finds elsewhere in the world. The problem is that the dissolution of culture both releases and betrays us. It gives us the space to create new styles, new gods and connections, but it denies us the strengths and talents to do it; for these are learned in relationships and community, and the dissolution of culture deprives us of them.

Our task, if we are to survive as creative human beings, must be to reject "a new sense of space" as an empty, barren, frozen wasteland—a void. In its place we must resolutely have the courage to affirm what is good and necessary in our past. We shall have to work with what we can and live with connections—doors leading to the past as well as windows open to the future.

I find that I must protest contemporary obsession with the inevitability of doom on the one hand, and delusive romantic fantasy that sadly arouses false hope on the other. However, it is the preoccupation with doom that may prove to be our greater danger. Many sensitive and intelligent people sadly subject themselves to a form of hypnosis that can render them passive victims of circumstance and impaled observers of events that they increasingly feel are past human control.

1

The setting was a dilapidated mansion located near the downtown area of a northeastern United States metropolis. It housed an urban commune whose members were former students, all whites, from families that were upper middle class in wealth or professional status.

I chatted in a basement room of the house with a twenty-three-year-old male member of the commune. He was a kind and sensitive young man who had had a superior education and was the son of a family distinguished nationally in public service.

"It's hopeless to work for change within the context of existing structures," he said. "I'm going to start engaging in acts of sabotage and destruction or else drop out of the struggle, go to another country and just have a ball before the end comes. I honestly believe there is only a short time left for any kind of viable human life on earth." The either-or of his alternatives seemed to shut out the humanistic revolution. Massive destruction and its consequent endangering of human lives, a preoccupation with seizing power instead of making positive changes in the quality of life, and "instant revolution" as a substitute for creating a new society: these constitute the very antithesis of the humanistic revolution. Hopeful alternatives would appear to be restructuring of primary institutions, creation of new institutions to meet human needs, and organizing people in order to change political structures.

The Goliath of institutional violence looms over us. To counter it simplistically with the tyranny of terrorism can become sordid, ugly, and viciously inhuman in itself, destroying people as well as the very heart of the revolution. On the other hand, to drop out of revolution—and selfishly pursue one's own desires and goals—can equally destroy people and contribute actively to the coarsening and degradation of the human spirit.

I affirm the necessity of humanistic revolution as an alternative to individual and mass death.

It is at present fashionable to pay attention to institutional structures, and ways that organizations affect people's lives, with little emphasis on individual responsibility. I am not at all disavowing the reality that our human lives are intertwined through institutions, or the profound influence upon us of the values that permeate them, when I reassert the human side of life.

Our involvement in the humanistic revolution needs to be understood as taking place within a permanent and continuing revolution for the transformation of individual lives (including our own) and the total life of society. Every man or woman is responsible to his conscience as well as to the revolution; the end that is sought is clearly inseparable from the means utilized to achieve it, and this may cause the individual to move against rigid conformities of revolutionary fashion in evolving an honest life style. For the concept of "chic revolution," with styles of violence dictated by money-making entrepreneurs—to whom humanistic revolution is as naïve as peace, justice or freedom—is a devastating irony.

If the revolution is not identifiable with integrity and compassion in the lives of revolutionary people, how can it illuminate the dark streets? A stinking parody of itself as an agent of dehumanization, instilling fear and utilizing facile propaganda, can only increase a malaise marked by cynicism and despair.

Shallow activism must, on the part of people committed to the revolution, be changed into a considerably deeper and more sophisticated sense of involvement. This calls for listening to people outside one's own ingrown and myopic claque as well as sober examination of self-righteousness in one's motives and actions. Communication with an "enemy," to change and enlist him in the humanistic revolution, is always to be sought instead of his harm or destruction.

Heroes and celebrities in the movement must desist from exploiting the cult of personality, allowing machismo to be quiet heroism in ordinary life situations instead of bravado performance on well-lighted stages. I have sat in jail cells in connection with highly publicized arrests in both the civil-rights and the peace movements, but I felt greater integrity when I was unobtrusively managing to communicate with people who had previously been opposed to black liberation or peace, instead of driving them into even greater polarization that snuffs out hope.

When I attended the performances of the Living Theater at Yale in 1968-69 I saw theater turning into revolution; on other occasions I have seen fantasies of revolution in the form of theater, played before the mass media with overacted gestures and role rhetoric. The mood has been fiery, romantic and cathartic. Costuming might have been credited to Givenchy. I have wondered when revolution is a luxury instead of a necessity; when it might provide a romantic high for someone who, when hungry, could always take time out to go home for a steak dinner.

Beyond mere "theater of revolution"—a performance before a crowd and camera—I found a more seriously intentioned playing with revolution. This was not for a crowd or camera at all, yet was based on the naïve assumption that revolution can be controlled by an elite (oneself and friends). A specific act of terrorism or violence (including accidental death in the bombing of a university building in the middle of the night) will be done to *those* people over there but will not come home to roost for *these* people over here. It reminded me of an Indian child playing with a cobra in a film by Satyajit Ray. Jerzy Kosinski's novel *Steps* caught the mood of this kind of playing: threads of suggested brutalization and violence, mental and emotional disarray, and psychic imbalance, all focusing finally on a man who is caught up in an actual revolutionary situation whose violent demands equal his self-induced anticipation.

The Kosinski portrayal of brutality belies the humanistic revolution. It seems to me the humanistic revolution is close to the meaning of authentic Christian experience in that it assumes a permanent revolution, within both the individual and society, never settling for a false peace,

146

constantly striving toward moral transformation as an action of loving. As Julius Lester has pointed out, nonviolence is not, then, a passive or servile posture (of not striking back if one is attacked or brutalized) but is filled with Gandhian assertive power, "with the force of one's soul."

From the humanistic view, revolution is seen as transcending conventionally corrupted power. It becomes a very way of life, seeking to correct the dehumanization inherent in all movements as well as the violence of the status quo. When they do not comprehend their own moral ambiguities, liberation movements primarily endeavor to achieve power, relegating self-knowledge to a place of secondary importance.

Yet if self-knowledge is properly seen as indispensable to both morality and survival—and, in the long run, these cannot be separated if human life is to be worth living—then certain truths become evident. One is that freedom is never simply part of a political or military game that is played in order to win it. Such a game is an abuse that profanes the humanistic meaning of freedom, tricking people into accepting a deadly substitute for it. Father Daniel Berrigan sent a tape to the Weathermen in 1970 urging them to disavow destruction and terrorism. He said that "no principle is worth the sacrifice of a single human being." Continuing, he noted that "when madness is the acceptable public state of mind we are all endangered from an infection in the air. The [peace] movement has at times been sickened by it too."

Too many people have died for the sake of the humanistic revolution to let it be easily destroyed. It is essentially a way of life, not a technique to shift power. The humanistic revolution seeks to replace the violence of the status quo with an order based on justice and freedom. Yet if it fails to incarnate in its own life the same qualities that it seeks for the greater society, it cruelly mocks its reason for existence, becoming a travesty in the eyes of people who desperately yearn for freedom. Humanistic revolution is concerned with living instead of killing. Therefore its goal is actual, not fantasied, change in the very quality and condition of human life. To avoid its betrayal requires the utmost honesty, courage and constantly renewed vision of human possibilities.

2

My education earmarked me to be "an American," "a white man" and "a Christian." It has taken the greater part of my life to unlearn the implications of what I was taught. I did not know that I have an allegiance to mankind that transcends my identity as "an American"; I belong to a race that defines me, not narrowly as "a white man," but as a creative and growing human being; philosophically, religiously and existentially, I am, because of historical circumstances of birth and environment (and personal decisions and commitments related to these), "a Christian." I was not born in Bombay; I was early offered Christ, but, oh, so vulgarly. I would have to learn that God was not really represented by a missionary (played by Katharine Hepburn) going down an African river in a white dress on an ancient barge, or even by that political missionary John Wayne at the Alamo.

There was a pantheon of heroes when I started to attend high school in the 1930s. In those days, before the Second World War, we believed that we had neither an unendurable social legacy of hate nor a frightening encounter that lay ahead with future shock. A Pearl Harbor was as remote a possibility as a magazine cover announcing "The Death of God." Ours was the world of the Roosevelts, Shirley Temple, Charles Lindbergh, Mae West, Will Rogers, Spencer Tracy, Lou Gehrig, Clark Gable, Ernest Hemingway and Babe Ruth, and, in the Sunday rotogravure section of the newspaper, the little English princesses, Elizabeth and Margaret Rose. Adolf Hitler seemed the Witch of the West. H. V. Kaltenborn brought us, over the radio, news of the witch. Our most fashionable anti-hero was Robin Hood.

I was not given an opportunity in junior high school, high school or college to establish a meaningful relationship with a black person. Yet these institutions spoke earnestly of giving me "an education." I was not taught American history or American literature but instead "white American history" and "white American literature." It is not alone black people who have a legitimate claim for reparations on the American culture. As a white boy and man I spent hours, days, weeks, months and years sitting in classrooms receiving not so much a minimal education as a false one. I was taught about a world that did not exist. How would I be able to cope with the real world? Perhaps it would be impossible. Maybe I would fight to the death people whose experience of life

—focus upon life and definition of it—was diametrically opposed to my own. War! Not love.

I was always taught that patriotism really meant "my country, right or wrong." But how, it was suggested, could it ever be wrong? History was shoehorned (taking a leaf from the Deuteronomists in the Bible) into neat categories. I was taught that war was justified if my country fought it. The church backed up this teaching. I was taught that blacks were crude and vulgar people called "niggers"—although one was never supposed to say that word, just to think it when looking upon a black face. I was taught that Native Americans were stupid, alcoholic, loutish bastards who had killed too many kind and courageous American (white) troops who were fighting for "our country." I was taught that Mexican-Americans were unspeakably dirty, smelly, unfortunate people who did manual labor and were always to be treated as children. This meant that they should be disciplined when necessary if they get out of line by acting uppity. Why didn't they learn to speak *English*? We mimicked their style of speech and laughed uproariously.

I was taught by U.S. war propaganda against the Japanese that they were a loathsome and dangerous people of "the yellow peril." Hi-ro-shi-ma. Hiró-shima. Hiroshí-ma. I doubt that I even heard the name while I was in high school. Years later, as an American student at an international seminar in Switzerland in 1955, I would live in a dormitory with a Japanese student, the first person from his land whom I had ever known as a person instead of an image. Following preliminary superficial discussions about the war, beneath polite smiles, we would finally reach a sufficiently profound level of friendship to permit our mutual confrontation of the Hiroshima event in human terms.

I was taught that foreign lands were distant and remote from my life. Then I read Alan Paton's *Cry, the Beloved Country*. South Africa was as near as today's newspaper headline. "It was Msimangu who had said, Msimangu who had no hate for any man, I have one great fear in my heart, that one day when they turn to loving they will find we are turned to hating. Oh, the grave and the sombre words." No place was distant any longer. Nothing was remote from my own thoughts. The words came closer and were from a young black man named Jesse Harris in Mississippi. "I was in solitary for 36 hours. The cell was 9 x 12, a 'sweatbox.' I was naked. The cell was a big steel vault in the ground, with no windows. They turned on heated air into the vault, and left it on all the time I was in the cell. . . . Then they put me back on the same road gang. After that one week, the guard pulled out a long hose pipe again and started to beat me one day without provocation. He struck me about 10 or fifteen times. I asked him why he had done that. He said: 'You are one of them smart-ass niggers. I don't like your ass.' "

I was taught that modern civilization was essentially good, incapable of committing horrors such as those of the past that were hidden in the pages of history books. The facts of Nazi concentration camps, revealed in sworn testimony in the Nuremburg Trials, cut against the limitations of my imagination.

The completely naked people went down a few steps which had been dug in the wall of the trench, scrambled over the heads of those who were lying there to the position that the SS man indicated. They lay down among the dead or wounded people; some stroked those who were still alive, and spoke quietly to them. Then I heard a succession of shots. I looked in the trench and saw how the bodies twitched; blood spurted from the necks.

.   .   .   .

Like pillars of basalt the dead stood there, pressed upright in the gas chambers. There was no room to fall or even to bend. Even in death one recognized families. They still held hands, embraced tightly in death, so that it was difficult to tear them apart to clear the chambers for the next charge. They threw out the bodies, wet with sweat and urine, smirched with feces, menstrual blood on their legs. Children's bodies flew through the air.

So the world was a jungle as well as a reminder of Eden. Life in it *today* was brutal, demanding, and sometimes evil beyond endurance. Why was I not taught this in school or church? Why had I not been prepared to live with the reality all around me and, indeed, inside my own heart? There would be so many voices from so many other places. My-lai (from *MY-LAI 4*, by Seymour Hersh): "I remember this man and his two small children, one boy and one girl, kept walking toward us on this trail. They just kept walking toward us, you know, very nervously, very afraid, and you could hear the little girl saying, 'No, no' in her Vietnamese tongue. The girl was on the right and the boy was on the left. All of a sudden, the G.I.'s just opened up and cut them down."

The world closed in upon me. How could I bear to hear these voices? What could I do to help the people who possessed them, or people like them, or people who survived them? Would my own, one day, be one of these voices?

As a youth I was taught that God was a remote, unyielding, powerful, unloving Thing up there somewhere, who did not really give a tinker's damn about any situation unless it happened, by horrible chance, to catch his celestial eye. Whereupon all hell broke loose, with vengeance visited upon hapless victims mercilessly and ceaselessly. Surely it was all a diabolical game of chance, for "niggers" were obviously damned by God from the outset, while I, for example, as a well-cared-for white boy, could simply develop my body and mind in proper ways and proceed to claim the world as my oyster.

The church occupied a central place in my young life. Many childhood memories revolve around it. I remember, on the evening when Orson Welles produced his classic radio broadcast about an imaginary Martian invasion of earth, that several friends and I attended a Sunday school supper at a cathedral. Bored, we concocted a plan to climb up inside the stone tower after everybody had departed in order to ring the bells of the cathedral. We thought it had the makings of a lark.

After supper we separated ourselves from the rest of the people and patiently waited in a remote hall for them to go home. We would go about our business when we were locked snugly inside the cathedral. Finally distant lights were turned off, doors bolted, and voices drifted away into the night. The radio program had begun its fateful broadcast—which would shortly result in national terror—when the four of us, alone inside the Gothic structure, moved swiftly through its dark interior. The splendid stained-glass windows appeared to be mere leaded spaces. The gigantic sanctuary with its stone altar seemed a treacherous inky expanse where evil spirits lurked ready to reach out with spiders' legs to pull us into a pit.

We found the door leading to the bell tower. The stairs were narrow and winding. We did not know what dead gargoyles or living church officials we might encounter face to face around the next turn of the stairs. Soon it became apparent we were being followed; I could hear the steady footsteps behind us. I told my companions to stop. We waited, holding our breath. The footsteps halted. We started again, tearing up the stairs, shouting at the top of our lungs to ward off evil spirits and confuse the demon in pursuit. We reached the bell tower, out of breath but ready to fight our pursuer. Only then did we realize the demon was our echo. We got down to the business of ringing the bells.

Unknown to us, the city was locked in deadly fear. To all intents and purposes, the Martians had landed. Switchboards of police stations, newspapers and broadcasting companies were swamped with desperate calls. Some people were in the streets, others had started out in their cars toward safety in the hills beyond the city. Suddenly the bells of the cathedral boomed out their note of warning and possible death. Doom! Despair! Those who had held back in cynicism, rational behavior, or perhaps a growing edge of anxiety, leaped headlong (we learned afterward) into the cauldron of public discombobulation.

154

Alarm! Man the barricades! To the walls! Doors of private houses and apartment houses were thrust open as men, women and children rushed into the night air. They looked toward the fortress of Almighty God, the Gothic stone pile of the cathedral, seeking reassurance or any sign of divine will. The cathedral presented the same face as always, betraying no evidence of God's intervention in men's affairs except for the fact that its mighty bell tower shook—heaved!—with the growing splendor of the clashing night bells ringing out over humanity in disarray. Elderly women fell to their knees in prayer. Men crossed themselves. Rosaries were in evidence. Tears streamed down faces.

Soon word started reaching the people that there *were* no Martians. The best thing to do was go home and get to sleep. Breathless with excitement about our achievement of ringing the bells, the four of us were now making our way down the winding stairway when we heard the ominous sound of police sirens. We realized that they were coming for us. Wondering if ringing the bells had been a major civic offense, and totally without knowledge of what had transpired outside in the city that night, we raced into the cathedral sanctuary mere footsteps ahead of a small army of police.

As I crouched behind the bishop's throne in the shadows, it seemed to me that church and state were not adequately separated. When the police made their way up the stairway to the bell tower we fled through a convenient herb garden of the cathedral toward our homes.

My childhood knowledge about God came partly from

occasional but memorably majestic invocations and benedictions delivered in a loud voice at school assemblies by clerics garbed in deathly black. Sunday school, of course, contributed basically to my knowledge of God by teaching me that he was an incredible combination of an old kingly white man with a long beard, the posthumous establishment hero Jesus (who was, the church taught me, tortured to death by the Jews), and "the Holy Ghost." The latter seemed to be A Big Wind. I saw it in action when the lighted candles on the church altar flickered during the mass. I knew it was caused by the Holy Ghost.

Acquisitiveness, I learned, was the medium; success the goal. Horatio Alger, a folk hero to me and my young friends, lived again in us. We had only to commit ourselves to acquisitiveness and worship success in order to be fulfilled as human beings on earth. We were drilled to recite "I am a success, you are a success, he is a success, she is a success, it is a success, we are a success, you are a success, they are a success." The key to the problem was work. Failure to work was a mortal sin; work itself offered absolution for lesser sins. Get *up* in the morning, get *out* into the arena of action, and work; your only chance is *now*. Although life might begin at forty (according to a popular book of the period), still every kid knew that he had to make it in school—get a scholarship, go to the right college, make the essential contacts with others on the way up, learn to know "who" as well as "what," be marked as a leader—get the right job, excel, get the right mate, live in the right neighborhood, don't waste a minute, know how to use the right words, know how to use the right silverware, know how to wear the right clothes, know how to wear the right face and hair, know how to laugh: Learn how, kid.

I was taught that women were housewives, mothers, schoolteachers, librarians, store clerks and waitresses. The church neatly bore this out by allowing women visibility before and after mass, as members of the Altar Guild, but clearly they were not deacons, priests or bishops. Women were bad drivers of cars, emotionally unstable (given to crying at weddings and funerals), silly, and intellectually inferior. Sex was something *done* to them. Whores were always female.

I was taught how to live according to the double standard. This instruction would prove to be indispensable for a middle-class, white American like myself. "Love thy neighbor," but be careful that he is the same in class, color, religion, political attitudes and life style. Sex, outside of coitus with one's legal mate inside one's own home, was, I learned, illegal. However, one could have infinite varieties of sex outside limits so long as one acted according to socially prescribed rules based on fundamental social deceit.

I was taught how respectable people paid every penny due the paper boy (myself for a period of time) and the grocer, but cheated on the income tax. I learned that one always invoked law if a "nigger" made the slightest infringement on order. Yet one always exceeded the speed limit by at least ten miles per hour, and remembered to leave a five-dollar bill on the passenger's seat after taking a driver's test if a new driver's license was sought with dispatch, and always paid off the neighborhood cops for security of a business establishment.

157

I was taught, in school and church, "Thou shalt not kill"; but soldiers were legendary heroes and "a just war" was sanctified, participation in it being a man's highest calling "for God and country."

3

Black rage. Nitty-gritty. Soul. Soul on ice. B. B. King. Aretha. Bessie Smith. Billie Holiday. Joe Louis. Muhammad Ali. Huey. Stokely. Coretta King. Angela Davis. Black consciousness. Black liberation. Black revolution. Black power.

In the midst of this I was white. Did I lynch, castrate, starve, burn, knife, hang, disembowel, rape and murder thousands and thousands of black people in America? Did I stand in the way of black progress, social equality and liberation in the United States?

In Los Angeles, listening to the people of Watts in 1965 during and immediately after their revolt, I found myself engaged in conversation with a young black man who said: "This wasn't a race riot. It was letting out a yell saying, 'We're still living, we're here, you've got to let us live like you do.' If they don't hear, the whole world will rise up. All poverty areas are going to rise. What blacks feel about whites is what has happened for the past five hundred years." I knew that I must study (and learn) *white* history. For my identity, which had seemed so secure when I confronted a black as "the invisible man," was now shattered.

A black woman in Watts, standing in the debris of

broken glass and smoking burned-out stores, told me: "A white cop stopped my car to give me a ticket the other day. He just stood there and told me, 'Get out, nigger bitch.' I'm not going to take that any more from the blue-eyed devil." I tried now to look deeply into the white experience but was unnerved by what I saw. I had been told it was all apple pie, prayers, cleanliness, decency, morality, righteousness, goodness, law, order, helping the poor, converting the natives; and it wasn't.

Ralph Ellison wrote in the prologue to his novel *Invisible Man*:

I am an invisible man. No. I am not a spook like those who haunted Edgar Allan Poe; nor am I one of your Hollywood-movie ectoplasms. I am a man of substance, of flesh and bone, fiber and liquids—and I might even be said to possess a mind. I am invisible, understand, simply because people refuse to see me. Like the bodiless heads you see sometimes in circus side-shows, it is as though I have been surrounded by mirrors of hard, distorting glass. When they approach me they see only my surroundings, themselves, or figments of their imagination —indeed, everything and anything except me.

He was right. The black man *was* invisible. But no more.

Was I therefore to be a masochist instead of the righteous ruler? What was to be my "role"?

It was not only as a white man but also as a priest that I participated in the civil-rights movement. I started out with a strict "role" based upon my self-image and how this was projected to other people in various situations. For example, I remember a Sunday morning in July 1965. There were other images in my consciousness too, those of the new people around me. I had never known anyone

159

like them before. I could not build any bridges between my past and present experiences.

I was living and working that summer in rural Alabama and Mississippi with four black men, all of them young yet veterans of the freedom movement in the Student Nonviolent Coordinating Committee. The five of us had shared a good deal of life in the past weeks—poverty, hunger, fatigue, police harassment, threats to our lives by white supremacists, and the seemingly endless rebukes of white people in ways large and small—the hate stare, the refusal to grant permission to drink out of a public fountain or use filling-station rest-room facilities, the smiling insult as if directed to a child. Now I wondered if we might conceivably share the mass.

We had spent the night in a rural shack made available to us by a poor black family. I got up early, found moldy bread and a bottle of beer in the icebox, placed them on a wooden table in the living room, and waited for the others to awaken. One man had spent the night with a white woman student he had brought back with him; he had to leave immediately to take her home, for it would be dangerous for them to be seen together any later in the morning. They departed in the car that we used for travel. Another of the men set out along a nearby highway to buy groceries.

I was left in the shack with two of the men and the young black woman who had spent the night with one of them. As we leisurely talked over cups of coffee I said that I hoped we might share the action of the mass and communion. I proposed to do this after the other two men had returned. The girl said that she could not participate because, in her belief, communion was holy—to be received only once or twice a year; sex was dirty, including the intercourse she had engaged in during the past night; she had been taught to keep communion and sex separated from each other. Soon one of the men became worried about the delayed return of the man who had gone out to buy food, and he set out to find him. Three of us remained. Then the man with the car came back. Another man in our group angrily attacked him for returning so late. The two swore at each other and fought in the room of that shack.

The wooden table was overturned, the beer spilling on the floor. The man who had returned with the car asked why the beer had been on the table. He knelt down, picked up the piece of bread, and tearing off the mold, ate it. I explained that I had wanted to share with them *this* part of *my* life, as I had shared so many parts of their lives with them. There seemed to be a feeling of sympathy for me. Not only was I white and older but there was this *other* separation too, this obsolete, or archaic, business of being a priest, something that none of them could talk about.

The others returned, peace was quickly made, I was once again absorbed into our fragile but very real community as if I were not separated at all ("You'll have to be a nigger like we are," one of them had said at the outset), and our common life continued as we ate toast and drank coffee. It seemed to me that, in a way I had neither designed nor sought, we received communion. But I wondered how I could relate this experience of my life to that other part of it in the church and the world as an

161

ordained and functioning priest. Church rules and regulations—indeed, the middle-class white cultural mores that were inseparable from them—seemed as remote as another century.

But what of my "role"? Would the institutional church feel this entire experience, including what I had wished to do with the bread and the beer, was wrong or illegal or blasphemous or even merely sadly isolated from reality? I was being changed; could I go back as if I were unchanged? I had been absorbed momentarily into a community that would shortly not exist for me, yet a terribly real one (and, if I died here, the last one I would know). Now I wondered if the community to which I would return—a parish church—could possess such intimate involvement (including the sweat, warts and ugly agony), depth of fellowship, or a kind of unnamed love that offered the totally shared experience of mutual risk in danger as well as a genuine caring for each other. For *here* we were prepared to die together in the cause of human liberation. My friends in the parish church would not, I knew, understand or readily express openness to these new and present friends, with their methods, language, attitudes and life style.

The decade of the 1960s was a strange period in which to be an ordained priest in the institutional church as well as an activist in the race movement. I recall setting out in September 1961 with twenty-seven other priests—all of us wearing spanking white clerical collars and black suits, carrying prayer books in our hands—on a freedom-ride bus inside the Deep South for what we called a "prayer pilgrimage." We were white and black; the night before climbing aboard the bus we had stayed in a dormitory of the Dryades Street YMCA in New Orleans, which John Howard Griffin has described in *Black Like Me*. Not easily falling asleep that night, I asked myself—as I would in later days, months and years—why we engaged in this action as a body of priests. Wouldn't our existential and/or institutional priesthood have been better served if we had taught and guided and prayed, and then twenty-seven laymen, exercising *their* priesthood, had boarded the freedom-ride bus? Any Christian active in the civil-rights movement knew his practice of religion was changed by his new experiences.

My human "role" was being eroded. Could I live freely as a human being without it? (But what, I asked myself, was it?) Another curious moment in contradictions of the priesthood today—this time from the peace movement—took place in a jail cell in Washington, D.C., in May 1970. I had been designated as the celebrant in a Peace Mass earlier that day, a service interrupted by the police, who arrested those of us taking part in it. This was my second arrest in seven months for participating in a Peace Mass inside the Pentagon. In the first one I gave the sermon, and a policeman with a bullhorn conducted an antiphonal and certainly unrehearsed dialogue with me, he tumbling out the words "You are under arrest," I uttering contrapuntal phrases, "If the salt has lost its taste, how shall its saltness be restored?" We were arrested on the charge that we were creating undue noise. At each Peace Mass the bread and wine for the service were placed on the cement floor; incense filled the air; bright Eucharistic vestments were directly next to military uniforms.

Now, inside jail, a man held the bottle of wine and the bread that were intended for the mass. He looked across the crowded cell toward me. "Here, Father, you consecrate the elements," he said. As the bread and wine were passed over to me, many questions about the meaning of the "role" of priesthood forced their way into my consciousness. (And my own "role" too, for how could my manhood and priesthood be related or separated?) Was it felt that I could invoke a kind of magic to change the wine into the blood of Christ? Was this action on my part seen as necessary in order for communion to be valid? If there were only laymen in the jail cell, would they feel it was impossible to have communion? Moments later, police entered the cell and took away the wine.

What the black liberation movement taught me is that I did not have to play any "role" as a white man *or* as a priest. It was not only my black brother who could be free. I, too, could taste freedom, liberation, release and a meaning that transformed my existence into a life. A "role" was a form of dehumanization of oneself and others.

In my freedom as a human being I could transcend roles that would imprison me—if I had enough courage to cut myself free from ties in the mind, the body, the personality and the society. I had the power to turn away from a white god who resided in temples of whiteness, white purity, white truth, white holiness. However, I knew that I would not be free if I turned to a black god who resided in temples of blackness, black purity, black truth, black holiness. Nor really did I want a green god, a red god, a yellow god or a blue god. Too, I did not want a white ghetto, a black ghetto, a green ghetto, a red ghetto, a yellow ghetto or a blue ghetto. With whatever breath was left in my body I would fight all of these ghettos. Because I knew that I could not speak of freedom as an individual if I could not live in a free society. "When you confront society and make clear that you will no longer exist as half a man, then they come out to destroy you," Rodolfo "Corky" Gonzalez, the Chicano leader, told me in Denver. "For their economy, their politics, even their sexual life, is threatened. Racism has made them paranoid. . . . We've committed our fifteen-year-olds to be men. After all, Fanon is right in a psychological sense: the slave cannot be free until he kills the oppressor. I say that you can do this intellectually, but you have to be strong enough. Hell, you're not even living unless you're involved in an action. You're not really living if you're getting callouses on your ass from watching TV or developing finger muscles by holding cans of beer."

Must I fight everybody? No. Anger, I was told by a lean black leader who had been tortured in jail, was almost as much a luxury as self-righteousness. I recognized that battles concern me only within the context of the humanistic revolution. I learned that humanness must assert itself over against dehumanization. How could I participate in this struggle if I were not human?

I would have to discover humanness with other people.

I have close black friends and white ones. Our blackness and our whiteness are vitally important in defining our individual humanness and our social relationship, but the blackness and whiteness finally do not separate us, but instead become the factor of blinding and painful humanity that links us. For I cannot truly enter the human experience if I do not comprehend (and partially live in) the black experience as well as the white experience.

The human experience is, in its fulfillment, a unity. However, this does not at all mean what we used to speak of as "integration." Whites must come to deal with the concept expressed by Julius Lester, writing in *Defiance*: "Even in the best of all possible worlds, it seems certain that a black nation will be desirable and necessary, for it is only in a separate nation that blacks will be able to be themselves. That sounds like such a little thing. It is, however, the essence of existence. Revolution has no other purpose than the creation of a society in which people can know and be themselves."

Survival is hard pragmatism. Freedom and liberation are hard as nails, not airy generalities. If a black abrasively rejects me—on the basis of my whiteness, not on the basis of knowing me as a person—it is inhuman and dehumanizing of me to react in protest, outrage, cries of self-pity and deprecation, and unholy preachment. ("The police beat me on the head after they handcuffed me," a black youth in Watts told me. "I know hate isn't going to do any good. But I'm not going to love a white. Nobody can define love to me. I might want to make love to a white, but I can't love a white.") We can, the two of us, maintain our humanness in the creative tension of separation. Isolated we will not be, for our mutual consciousness of one another is a burning thing. Do not misunderstand me: I speak of the deliberate decision of wanting to maintain our humanness together *and* working to do this in the creative tension of separation. This is neither separatism nor indifference. If we seek this mutual goal, that requires one another, we can remain human within tactical separation. Of course, with still other blacks, I am joined in the open celebration of friendship and shared struggle to unite black experience with white experience. We do this in the belief that it is the human experience that defines, kills and resurrects us.

4

I revisited the city after an absence of five years. I discovered that it curiously resembled a gigantic and finely detailed map, broken asunder into many small fragments.

I was walking late at night in the city. "It is dangerous," a friend had said. "There are stabbings and muggings, and one risks his life. The city at night is a jungle where one might step on a cobra."

Now, past midnight, I walked alone on a dimly lighted street. There was not another sign of human life. The collar of my coat was turned up to keep the stabbing icy wind from my throat and chest. My eyes watered, my feet were near freezing, but I rejoiced in the awareness of being in the city at night again.

The figure approached me from a distance of two

blocks. It could be a Martian or an Asian, man or woman, black or white, man or child, Catholic or Waldensian, Jew or Greek: I walked toward it, fear moving slowly up my legs, down my arms, gripping my abdomen. Would I die here alone in the wasteland of this frozen street at night under a moonless sky?

No. I could run. Run! Fly! I walked ahead, allowing no break in the rhythm of my stride. (One must not reveal a semblance of weakness before the enemy.) The figure was now one full block closer to me.

It was a man. It was a black man. The sound of the wind began to be fragmented by his footsteps on the pavement. He stole a glance at my face, I stole a glance at his. The two bodies moved toward each other as if choreographed on a lifeless stage that extended as far as the eye could see.

No sound came from the figure's mouth. I repressed a cough that had its combustion deep inside my chest, though a feather twirled sadistically in my throat. I glued my eyes straight ahead; so did the figure, presently coming abreast of me. Could one say "Hello" to a lone human being past midnight in heaven or hell? "Hi" to a fast-moving body hurling past oneself in orbit around the earth?

I said nothing. The figure—a whirling universe encased inside its head—topped by an Afro and a black cap—passed by me in silence. Insanely and pragmatically, the two bodies withdrew from each other on the wind-swept street that could have been a designer's set for the human heart.

Distance replaced the closeness that had never existed. The encounter had been as impersonal as two cars passing each other on a highway in the night: the tiny dots of light drawing closer, closer, nearly here, now upon each other, then past, and suddenly there is darkness again.

I wanted to see particular friends again, walk as I had used to do along certain streets, look upon places that held private meaning for me, and match my present moods with the hopeful re-creation of past ones.

I had loved the city, experienced love within it, wept and laughed inside its walls, vigorously waged battle for my ideas in its forums, knowingly accepted the rage of controversy, and felt the sickening malaise of despair as well as the stirring of new force with hope again.

Did revisiting the city awaken inside me feelings of optimism or pessimism? Neither.

I was reminded of a lengthy private conversation that I had had in Rome several years ago with the sensitive, renowned and extremely down-to-earth Cardinal Bea. He had acted as confessor to Pope John XXIII and was one of the fathers of the ecumenical movement. His death, in 1968, saddened Christians throughout the world. He told me during our talk that he considered himself neither an optimist nor a pessimist, but a realist.

Cardinal Bea's words have deeply affected my thinking about life. An optimist, it seems to me, has the outrageous temerity to wear rose-colored glasses in order not to see the depths and details of stark black-and-white reality. A pessimist, I feel, is sick unto death in his failure to perceive dimension and perspective; he refuses to see beyond his own feet and a few inches of space surrounding them on the ground.

A realist throws away rose-colored glasses, straightens his shoulders and looks freely about him in all directions. He wants to see whatever there is to see, in relation to other people and things as well as to himself. A realist alone comprehends hope. Optimism is as antithetical to authentic hope as pessimism. Hope is rooted in realism.

Revisiting the city, I tried to cast off optimism and pessimism alike, for I find them to be ultimately death-dealing and therefore obscene. As an observer-reporter, I wished to work within the context of realism and its companion, objectivity. On this basis I might be able to proceed with hope. If I were able to see people and conditions as they really were, I knew that my diagnosis had an excellent chance of being correct.

"We've decided to live with it." A stocky white man in his forties, who earned his living by means of the advertising trade, chatted with me over a cocktail in one of the city's prestigious restaurants. Soon a rare steak would be served us. The ad man was an old friend whom I had not seen since 1964.

"Nothing is being *really* tried in the city," he said, lighting a cigarette. "We're on a collision course. You see, there is a sense of no hope." His eyes were deadly serious behind the folded skin of his quizzical and eternally smiling face.

"Make it with Tanqueray," called my friend to a

waiter after he had placed our orders for martinis in a hotel dining room. I had met my black militant friend in 1963 when he was one of the shrewdest, coolest activist-intellectuals I had ever known. Now his mood was a looser one; his eyes were not so tense, his body not so wiry.

"Revolution?" He laughed. "It seems to be revolution-in-reverse. The people who used to see each other don't do it anymore. The hopeful talk and the plans for change. You remember—something was going to happen. Everybody knew it. All the pressure was building up. Something completely new and different *had* to happen, man. But it didn't."

I was in a demographic section of the city, the Jewish section. "Little Jerusalem" I had once heard a white Protestant student derisively call it. I was dining with friends whom I had not seen in many years.

"My greatest fear is that repression may lead to a police state," Doris, the wife of an accountant, said. "It *could* happen here. They say blacks would be first, but I don't know. Do you realize how *closely* Jews were integrated into the German society at *all* levels? Most people do not understand this. It simply takes a demagogue, an event like the Reichstag fire, official propaganda, and arousing latent prejudices. Don't ask me *how* they do or *why*. We've thought of moving to Israel, but it's impossible. The children must go to school here."

She asked me if I wanted something more to eat.

"The blacks. *Are* they anti-Semitic? I can't understand it. What does it mean?"

It was Saturday morning in the city. I walked through the downtown streets toward the biggest department store. It had been the citadel of shopping, the meeting place of interesting people. I would revisit it.

Overhead clouds in the sky were reflected slowly moving against the façade of a tall building. On the pavement with me were very few people. Where had all the people gone? Presumably the middle-class blacks and whites were off somewhere in a suburb. Around me were poor people, black and white. Carrying brown-paper shopping bags, they moved slowly and without enthusiasm. Grinning lifelessly at us from store windows were mannequins wearing glittering dresses and mod suits that seemed to mock an elderly, hungry-looking white man ahead of me and a heavy black woman surrounded by eight children impatiently crowding around her. A white youth thrust a newspaper into my hands; it was a periodical of Gay Liberation. A black youth held up a Panther newspaper.

Children were everywhere, making me think of a Children's Crusade. Bands of them, almost always without an accompanying adult, wandered the streets aimlessly. They moved through stores, jostled lone pedestrians on the sidewalk, gestured wildly as they peered into shop windows, and stopped to hear rock music being played through loudspeakers outside music stores. They ogled theaters advertising pornographic movies and laughed. I wondered for a moment if the Chinese Cultural Revolution had come to the city.

When I reached the great store I walked through its

departments, one after another. A dozen children giggled near me as they passed by. I saw miles of furniture and lamps, kilometers of dishes, plates, cups and saucers. Where were the people?

One morning I walked up the blood-giving artery of the city, the avenue that feeds thousands of automobiles into the downtown area every morning, then releases them again at night. People congregated outside a corner liquor store, talking in small groups. A lady sat reading a magazine in the box office of a burlesque house. Grotesquely crumpled pages of a derelict newspaper blew against the curb.

I walked more briskly now, searching for an old coffeehouse theater that I used to know. It was a ramshackle, often condemned, always troubled building that had given us a roof for a primitive, indigenous people's theater that was exciting in a razor's-edge sense of bypassing convenient relevance. Approaching a familiar corner, I looked down the street. The building had vanished; only a vacant dirt lot remained. The theater had not possessed sufficient magic to save itself.

My God. What if my old apartment house had vanished too? Alternately running and walking, I hastened toward it. Private houses and apartment houses in its vicinity had visibly deteriorated. It had always been a section consigned to what society called failure and dying. Yet I had known liberation and joy in its lack of pretense, open and defenseless relationships between people, and a sense that one was momentarily spared the ruthlessness of an aggressive society that encroached upon human sensibilities as it automatically devoured time, space and people.

My apartment had been at the back of the old house on the third floor. As it did not have an elevator, one walked the creaking, faded carpeted stairs that allowed no privacy of movement, day or night, to any of the inhabitants. When I came near it, it hurt me to look toward the site of the apartment house. I wanted it to still be there. I caught my breath as I turned my head. It was there.

Students on the sprawling urban campus, a block away from the old apartment house, appeared the same as their counterparts of five years before. An asphalt campus inside a city is seldom ever a dashing or very chic place. Its style is arcane, hidden from merely desultory eyes or a casual look.

Not long before, a student had been shot to death in broad daylight in the middle of this campus. I walked to the area where the death had occurred. I saw only an army of students moving briskly between classes. It was a nonviolent army engaged in the higgledy-piggledy craft of education and the tender art of living. Sex stirred easily on the campus as it always had. ("But where do they *go?*" a nonacademic visitor had once asked me, looking at hundreds of milling young men and women who did not possess rooms except in their parents' homes.) There was no doubt that a new campus crisis today would give way to a newer one tomorrow. I studied the vigor and simple caring of the students who surrounded me. Peace symbols seemed to be everywhere—on their

174

jackets, around their necks, painted on their books. I was an anonymous older man, unknown and forgotten, invisible within a mass.

Friends in a rich and impeccably fashionable suburb asked me to visit them.

The view from their bridge was a startlingly different one. They had everything, it seemed, yet spoke of needs. "We need to talk with people like you who have ideas and live outside," a man told me.

"It's comfortable and we feel secure—knock on wood," a woman said. "But we don't know what's *happening*. We need deeper meaning. It's scary."

"I've developed one voice and manner of speech to use at home with my parents," a sixteen-year-old high-school girl confided in me, "and another voice and way of speaking at school with my friends." I told her that she should be careful or else she might develop throat cancer. She made a funny face at me. "I'm *definitely* going to move out," she said, "when I reach eighteen. Women's Lib is going to begin right *here*."

Early on Saturday morning I visited the outdoor Eastern Market. I thought this was the best place in the whole city. Farmers sold their produce in stalls: carrots, chickens, lettuce, apple juice, rabbits, potatoes, squash, beets, pumpkins, homemade breads, cakes, pies, eggplants, spices and greens.

Prices were low. Rich, middle class and poor were here together. Some families purchased food for a week, transporting it home in carts. I selected a small and lovely plant for my transient room. The plant and I would breathe together the air of our shared space and become environmental friends.

"There's a rise in crime—a feeling of no safety and personal danger," a priest told me. "Use of drugs is up," a doctor said. "It terrifies me. I see no end in sight. I work in a clinic. You should see the marks on people's arms when they roll their sleeves up. I feel the problem is overwhelming." "You're a beautiful person," a student said over a cup of coffee on the urban campus. "If you need a joint, just let me know. I know the underground." "I live in a commune where we share all of our ideas," a black girl told me. "I feel so good to be alive. I want to do so many things. My whole life has a single purpose and I found it in my blackness."

People inhabiting the different fragments of the city's gigantic map did not know each other. Many of them disliked or feared something mysterious—the images of other people.

Revisiting the city, I felt my life caught in a balance. Various friends of mine had died since I had gone away. I knew that others might die before I came back again. I could perceive the possibility of my own death. The watch strapped to my wrist counted the beats of the blood inside me. Tick. Tick. Tick. I saw a clock on a building; it absorbed passing moments with the routine fury of a python. I knew that the feeling of my control over life was a delusion. I heard a jet plane in the sky, yet I was being hurled ahead through life faster than its metal body.

Standing on a street in the city, surrounded by people going their own way, I momentarily felt that I was a stranger. I could be standing on a corner of medieval Florence or ancient Corinth, the Tudors' London or the Aztecs' most splendid city. Yet I was not. I stood in this specific area of time and space.

I was buoyed by a strong sense of hope. Despite the city people's sense of alienation and apartness from each other, I saw them as a whole. They had the capacity to choose life over death. They could discover and hold a common vision of creative possibilities for humanness. I looked at the city's people with my naked eyes, not through rose-colored glasses of illusory optimism or with the opaque despair of pessimism. Realism gave me solid grounding for hope.

Now I knew that when I left I would not be able to leave the city's people behind as I previously assumed I had done. I had learned a basic truth of these times. The city has no walls.

5

Despite my belief that the humanistic revolution is close to the meaning of authentic Christian experience, legitimization of indifference to human suffering is freely offered by the insensitivity of organized religion. Turning its back on the demands of conscience, the church seems callously committed to the acquisition and maintenance of temporal power. With relentless irony, it stands as a power institution on the side of the status quo instead of for human liberation.

More people are killed by indifference than bullets; the worst form of violence is not explosives but simply not caring about what happens to people. Yet Christian consciences have fallen into sad disuse, evidence of personal and institutional forms of violence discernible on all strata of American life.

James Baldwin, writing in *Notes of a Native Son*, spoke of "the zeal of those alabaster missionaries to Africa to cover the nakedness of the natives, to hurry them into the pallid arms of Jesus and thence into slavery." George Jackson, in one of his prison letters in *Soledad Brother*, wrote: "Right behind the expeditionary forces (the pigs) came the missionaries and the colonial effect is complete. The missionaries, with the benefits of Christendom, school us on the value of symbolism, dead presidents, and the rediscount rate. The black colony lost its conscience to these missionaries. Their schools, their churches, their newspapers and other periodicals destroyed the black conscience and made it almost impossible for us to determine our own best interest." The church has long supported imperialism, colonialism and war by means of its social actions and financial investments. It has lost sight of love in its pragmatic confrontation with the dollar sign, establishment politics and the social balance of power.

I recall an extraordinary incident that is illustrative of the end result of the church's teaching.

Ten people, including myself, stood in a circle. The setting was the foyer of an auditorium in a midwestern U.S. city. Inside the adjoining hall a major Protestant denomination was opening its church convention. Each of us within the circle wore an armband reading "41,791." This was at that time the official number of U.S. war dead in Vietnam. We took turns reading aloud the names, published in the *Congressional Record*, of American casualties. Every half hour we knelt to pray silently for a moment, remembering also the Vietnamese war dead, whose names we did not know. A crowd of Christian delegates was milling around the outside of the circle. Suddenly a middle-aged clergyman, faithfully attending his church's convention, broke angrily into the circle. "What has this to do with God?" he asked.

Indeed. I felt that the clergyman was honest in his reaction, given the background of his teaching and professional indoctrination. He had long learned from the church that God is concerned with "religion"—not the world. With "worship"—not life. With "ethics" (of the Ten Commandments, understood literally)—not the daily police blotter. With "morality," that is to say, s-e-x —but certainly not war, poverty, racism and (that dirty word) politics.

Let us take a look at s-e-x in light of the humanistic revolution and the ribald but guiltier-than-thou urban America of Mae West and Billy Graham ("pornography is part of an underworld conspiracy to undermine the morals of America"), *Playboy* and Miss America.

Is sex becoming more or less human? With a new permissiveness, life in communes, serious questions about male chauvinism raised by Women's Liberation, Gay Lib moving into public view, archaic sex laws undergoing critical public scrutiny, and a profound search for sexual openness and honesty, is hypocrisy being leveled and a newer humanistic life style introduced to the majority of people?

There are signs. Perhaps they point to answers.

"Without talking jargon or politics, you've got to say that revolution is necessary for any woman who opens her eyes, and sees what her 'womanly role' really amounts to," a twenty-three-year-old married woman living in a commune told me last year. She explained that her view was not "anti" male. "Hopefully, we're redefining both sexual roles. We want to free the man who is losing his humanity too, slaving away for higher productivity, bringing his paycheck home to the little woman."

Another woman in the same commune agreed with her. "*I'm* oppressed," she said, "in terms of what society has defined for me as feminine, and what I should be in order to be a woman. . . . What an American woman should want to be, we're taught, is just a wife and mother. In the nuclear family, this makes her essentially a slave, and the best consumer American capitalism can find. . . . Here in the commune, men and women cook, clean, wash the dishes, mow the lawn, and build things. The women all want to take a course in car mechanics because we're sick of being exploited by car garages. Some of us want to take karate."

Gay Liberation as well as radical lesbianism within the context of Women's Liberation are creatively probing the meaning of identity as against socially accommodated roles. The humanistic revolution is committed to sexual freedom as an essential quality of a human life. This does not mean sexual exploitation. However, it does mean the opportunity to live a unified life in a dissenting individual life style instead of a socially prescribed mosaic existence imposed by social demands for outward conformist adherence to rigid patterns of acceptable human and sexual experience.

In his article "What It Means to Be a Homosexual," written for *The New York Times Magazine*, Merle Miller noted:

Laws discriminating against homosexuals will almost surely be changed. If not this year, in 1972; if not in 1972, in 1976; if not in 1976 . . . Private acceptance of homosexuals and homosexuality will take somewhat longer. Most of the psychiatric establishment will continue to insist that homosexuality is a disease, and homosexuals, unlike the blacks, will not benefit from any guilt feelings on the part of liberals. So far as I can make out, there simply aren't any such feelings. On the contrary, most people of every political persuasion seem to be too uncertain of their own sexual identification to be anything but defensive. Fearful. And maybe it is contagious. Prove it isn't.

Social strictures upon certain people in particular sex roles have been extremely cruel. For example, take the unmarried pregnant woman. She has long been subjected to outrageous social judgments. I recall a college woman, pregnant and unmarried, who was forced to leave the campus amid rumors, lies and considerable personal suffering. She learned in the process that she was rejected by sorority *sisters* and house*mother*; there was simply neither love nor understanding, compassion nor the possibility of human communication. Her own family thought first of their own social position in a small town, and the implicit threat made upon it by her condition, rather

181

than her well-being or happiness. Take the pregnant woman seeking an abortion. I remember a college woman who seriously contemplated taking massive doses of LSD because she had heard a rumor that it might help to induce a miscarriage. She was distraught and entertained more than mere passing thoughts of suicide. Her puritanical parents had taught her to think of abortion as being outside the realm of decency or possibility.

In this electrically charged sexual atmosphere fraught with repression and guilt, the so-called pornographic book or movie has become culturally noteworthy. For some it marks rebellion against authoritarian pressures, even becoming a symbol of intellectual or artistic liberation. For others it unlooses secret or hidden personal feelings. However, Kate Millett in *Sexual Politics* sounds a warning:

Since the abatement of censorship, masculine hostility (psychological or physical) in specifically *sexual* contexts has become far more apparent. Yet as masculine hostility has been fairly continuous, one deals here probably less with a matter of increase than with a new frankness in expressing hostility in specifically sexual contexts. It is a matter of release and freedom to express what was once forbidden expression outside of pornography or other "underground" productions, such as those of De Sade. As one recalls both the euphemism and the idealism of descriptions of coitus in the Romantic poets (Keats's *Eve of St. Agnes*) or the Victorian novelists (Hardy, for example) and contrasts it with [Henry] Miller or William Burroughs, one has an idea of how contemporary literature has absorbed not only the truthful explicitness of pornography, but its anti-social character as well. Since this tendency to hurt or insult has been given free expression, it has become far easier to assess sexual antagonism in the male.

I had always accepted the fact that pornography was to be found in the eye of the beholder. But now along came, as Exhibit A in the sex wax museum, the "sex" film. The exhibitor beheld it as pornographic. He probably would have made money even without the help of various religious leaders whose florid denunciations (offered, of course, without their ever having seen the "sex" film) caused box-office grosses to soar sensually.

Since s-e-x in our culture is a pervasive word, probably also including the kitchen sink of the psyche, the "sex" film is Freud's umbrella. A more permissive social attitude toward other people's sex lives, with a clearer understanding of their practical variations, would vastly aid society as well as the individuals inside it. Any form of sexual practice between consenting adults, including husbands and wives (who, for example, at the present time in forty-eight of the states, cannot legally engage in oral intercourse), ought not to be described by professional moralizers as being outside society's pale of respectability.

Sexual repression is fraught with menacing social implications, the more so when accompanied by sweaty self-righteousness directed against other people's actual and self-accepted sexual practices. Certain sex arbiters, including highly publicized religious spokesmen, seem to forget the universality of sexual experience as a part of everyone's human life. Such sex arbiters are largely responsible for the fact that appearances may not be what they are supposed to be. For many people have felt that they were compelled to disguise the realities of their sexual motivation and behavior. This has brought us face to face with the "sex" film, a mirror of people's fantasies and suppressed desires.

When unabashedly explicit Danish films concerning a sex fair in Copenhagen opened in the United States in 1970 I decided that I should see one. The published reviews referred to past police raids on houses showing the movie and frankly labeled the film as pornography. I was conscious of Rabelaisian undertones as I stood in line before the box office in broad daylight waiting to purchase my ticket. What would people say? A reverend struggling to understand that same world in which Christ lived and died? A "rebel priest" raising hell once again? An adult male going to see a movie of his choice? Now I moved inside the theater. Everybody looked at everybody else. This was the show within the show. For everybody seemed to be making judgments about everybody else. Sex maniacs! Dirty young men! Dirty old men! Nymphomaniacs! Whores! Voyeurs! Then the lights dimmed and the movie began.

After it ended I walked outside the theater, adjusting my eyes to the glare of the sunlight. Moving up the street, I thought about the movie. I was glad that an adult desiring to see it could do so in a public and matter-of-fact way. However, instead of acknowledging the irrefutable fact of mystery, we had got simply the clinical movie close-up; in the place of expert sex education for children, which could lead to happier and better lives for millions of adult men and women, we had the sensational advertising and mystique of the "sex" movie. I recalled the strange audience reaction that I had observed at a showing in New York of the forerunner of this "sex" film, *I Am Curious, Yellow,* a movie that depicted nude male and female bodies as well as the simulation of intercourse. When the audience filed out at the conclusion of the film nobody spoke. I had observed such a phenomenon only once before at the conclusion of a film. It was a Rossellini film concerning a young German boy who had committed suicide. One heard only the shuffling of hundreds of feet, without the sound of a single human voice. I could not gauge the depth or precise nature of the threat that racked the audience on either of the two occasions. In the case of the Rossellini film it was more understandable: a young boy's profound despair had led him to take his life. But in the case of *I Am Curious,* was it simply that a direct public confrontation with sex— after all the publicity foreplay—had curiously unnerved the battle-weary, used-to-being-teased movie audience?

In human anxiety, sex plays a central role. Yet it must be remembered that sex is a part of life, not the whole of it. So sex cannot be isolated from the rest of life if one wishes to make sense out of it.

Most people are not looking for sex alone at the exclusion of love. In fact, the absence of love in sexual relationships can sadly heighten a sense of loneliness and apartness. It is ironically the feeling of loneliness growing out of mobility, rootlessness and impersonal urban living that heightens the search for love, which can manifest itself in an attempt to grasp it quickly and sometimes desperately in sex. However, sex needs love to fulfill it, giving it dimension and meaning beyond—or within—it-

185

self. Love means caring, responsibility, tenderness, relationship, the expression of feeling—therefore humanness.

One day I was chatting about sex with a student. As our conversation became more intimate he told me about a young woman with whom he had enjoyed sexual intercourse. Their experience had been a pleasant one, and, he told me that at its conclusion, he had said to her, "Thanks for not saying 'I love you.'" He was looking straight at me and his eyes never blinked. For a moment I felt sorry for him. But then I realized that the young man—and certainly the young woman too—mistrusted words, and that words are conventionally used to say the opposite of what one feels.

It is perhaps the ultimate tragedy when the sense of joy about life is lost by anyone. Bankruptcy in the consideration of sex becomes clear precisely when a sense of joy about sex is wiped out. All is not tragic. There is laughter; and it need not be a laughter of madness, it can be a laughter marked by joy, simplicity and sharing. Sex is many things: pleasure, responsibility, procreation, ecstasy, release, drudgery, fantasy and reality. Many people take it entirely too seriously—and therefore not seriously enough.

One finds oneself in astonishing situations of sexual candor and/or confession. Indeed, one can take nothing for granted sexually about anybody.

I was standing one morning in the check-out line of a supermarket, where I had gone to buy groceries. A Methodist minister, who was in his twenties and referred to himself as avant-garde, joined me. He was holding in his hands a head of lettuce, two pounds of ground meat, a package of Duz and a quart of vitamin D milk. We chatted as the line slowly moved, and I realized that he was speaking in an autobiographical vein.

"You'd never believe it," he said, "but I was a virgin until I was twenty-five. I sure as hell have made up for it ever since." A man standing directly ahead in the line coughed. The woman behind us touched her hair. The minister shifted the shopping items in his hands. Standing alongside a display of *Woman's Day* and Certs, I smiled politely, mentally fending off bad vibrations. "Puritanical parents, small town, and then the Methodist seminary, you know," he continued. "I'm great now. I have it all the time. I don't think I'll get married. I'm afraid of hang-ups." The check-out line slowly moved ahead.

Is sex becoming more or less human? The answer seems to be an individual one. People in the process of becoming more human tend to bring sex into the framework of the humanistic revolution. Freedom, not license, is its principal guideline for sex. License assumes freedom when there is instead slavery to self; freedom willingly takes on the self-limitation of responsibility for another life and other lives.

"Morality" is one of the least understood and most widely used words in this society's lexicon. The humanistic revolution has still a long way to go in communicating its meaning concerning sex and freedom, war and peace, identity and liberation.

6

Revolution that seeks to achieve the humanistic society rather than merely political transfer of power, and comprehends its own moral ambiguities in an intellectual and moral effort to achieve integrity, is close in theory to the meaning of authentic Christian experience. This is so because it assumes a permanent condition of revolution, within both the individual and society, constantly striving toward moral transformation as an act of loving.

However, there is an image of God that is antithetical to such a humanistic revolution. It is the image of God who remains *up there*, where he is immaculately clean, unsweaty, apolitical, asexual, puritanical in taste, exalted *and* deeply "religious." He is on the side of law and order, an unchallenged status quo, and entrenched privilege.

The custodian of this image of God remains the establishment, or institutional, church. While it sometimes retains the rhetoric of primitive Christianity, it stands opposed to its meaning in practice. Organized religion is a primary factor in the maintenance of the sociopolitical-economic establishment. It does not adequately assist in the radical transformation of individual lives—from selfish participation in the unchanged order to genuine religious sensitivity and sacrifice—but, with a maddeningly obdurate conformity to norms of institutional self-interest, becomes an actual obstacle to such conversion.

This custodial role of the church is as significant, from an intellectual and cultural standpoint, for an atheist or an agnostic as it is for a practicing religionist, because of the implications of the existence of such a God (and the establishment church as his custodian) for every aspect of modern society.

James Francis Cardinal McIntyre, retired Roman Catholic archbishop of Los Angeles, provided an example of this role when, in an interview reported by the Associated Press (Sept. 12, 1970), he spoke out against campus revolt (my italics): "These policies that have been manifested in the past few years are in reality *a revolution against Almighty God because it is a revolution against the authority of the university, the state and police.* All of these are authorities that command respect from people. The situation is alarming." The Associated Press, reporting an interview the prelate had given in Baker, Oregon, continued: "Cardinal McIntyre said he believes the Catholic Church and religion in general have a grave responsibility to restore to the people the realization of the existence of God and *the obligation to obey His law, the law of the country, and the authority established in every locality.* He said the true spirit of all religion is to obey Almighty God, and disobedience is manifested in riots."

Such an equation of God *on the side of* the institutional status quo is as indefensible and patently absurd as limiting one's view of Jesus Christ to that of an angry prophet overturning the money changers' tables inside the temple. Zealots have a historical and psychological tendency to create God or gods in their own image, out of their own needs and for their own purposes—and to do this in the conveniently accessible name of "Almighty God."

189

The question of patriotism versus religion is not a new one. It is ageless and universal. On "Honor America Day" in Washington, D.C., on July 4, 1970, Billy Graham said: "Why should I, as a citizen of heaven and a Christian minister, join in honoring any secular state? . . . Jesus said, 'Render unto Caesar the things that are Caesar's.' The Apostle Paul proudly boasted that he was a Roman citizen. The Bible says, 'Honor the nation.' " Does one's faithfulness to religion also demand one's unswerving loyalty to the state? Does one's worship of God include fealty to the established order?

Amos spoke to Israel:

> Take away from me the noise of your songs;
> to the melody of your harp I will not listen.
> But let justice roll down like waters,
> and righteousness like an everlasting stream.

At a time of peril we turn increasingly to the prophets of the Bible. For we seek guidance in the midst of perplexity, and examples of national pride and the justice of God thousands of years ago as of today. Religion is concerned with men's lives and the world of human values and decisions. So it involves itself, by its very nature, in the overarching questions of society, poverty and war.

Recently it was implied by some men, including Spiro W. Agnew, the Vice-President of the United States, that to protest against the Vietnam war was to give comfort to the enemy—in a sense, then, to engage in a form of treason. We must respond to this implication clearly and fearlessly. For the implication overlooks the honest and passionate conviction of many that the Vietnam war was destroying the very fabric of American life and coarsening its remaining sensitivities; that it was turning us inexorably from possible justice and peace to a long, and maybe fatal, course of militarism, chauvinism, limited-range expediency without the discipline of moral integrity, and even human holocaust. In light of such a conviction, to end this war—and prevent the start of other wars, thereby dealing with the cause of war itself in modern society—was imperative to preserve democratic processes and offer a hope of peace and justice to the world.

This burning question of the humanistic revolution is also a religious one.

We have spent billions of dollars in the tragically ironical destruction of a people we had the hypocrisy to say we wished to save. The rest of the civilized world asked us to examine the American conscience—many people, at home and abroad, doubted its existence—following the disclosure of war atrocities. The government of South Vietnam, our ally, has been a bastion of fascism with its denial of freedom of the press, freedom of political dissent, academic freedom and freedom of speech.

Isaiah said, "I am a man of unclean lips and I dwell among a people of unclean lips." We cannot condemn others if we withhold the severest form of self-criticism. We cannot allege our moral purity or absence of moral failures. We cannot ever join with those who would say "My country, right or wrong." Instead we might wish to repeat the words of Albert Camus: "I should like to be able to love my country and still love justice."

In his inaugural address in January 1969 President

Richard M. Nixon asked all the American people to lower their voices—to desist from tantrums and the use of epithets and to try to hear one another. We must soberly, quietly and reflectively examine this in light of subsequent events. For the President's appeal came before the Vice-President of the United States raised *his* voice.

Perhaps the Vice-President was unaware of the growing fear and anxiety felt by many people in religion, along with large numbers of intellectuals, students, black people, Chicanos, Native Americans and poor white people. In other words, there was emerging a minority fear and anxiety in America. It was only exacerbated by angry attack and reiterated reminder that there existed a silent majority that wielded the nation's power. Minorities certainly did not need to be reminded of that. What they needed, in addition to equal rights and institutional justice, was assurance that the silent majority did not regard them as queer, subversive, insolently negative and likely converts to be "saved" by coerced inclusion into the majority.

A growing number of people in America have come to live in an increased dread of repression, the breakdown of freedom to dissent, and even punishment, in the form of possible incarceration in prison or prison camps. Perhaps the Vice-President found this absurd. But the people who expressed such fears found it absurd that, for example, the McCarran Act was still law, despite the recent American experience of detention camps for Japanese-Americans during World War II and the loss of their property and civil rights.

The Vice-President did not allay any fears when he

singled out for criticism what he chose to term "the glib, activist element who would tell us our values are lies" and then proposed "to separate them from our society with no more regret than we should feel over discarding rotten apples from a barrel." How did the Vice-President propose to affect this "separation from society"? The Nazi experience is still too close to allow any such reference to be anything but unnerving.

If the silent majority (I wonder what this curious public-relations term means), dwelling in the most affluent nation in the history of the world, cannot hear legitimate criticism of the American life style without lashing out in truculent defensiveness, then the fearful and basically creative minorities must be made to feel ever more fearful. If articulated concern about the integrity of the American way of life is to be vilified, and a public accounting of mutual failure callously dismissed, then youth might well have reason to doubt its capacity to work within this system, which they know otherwise is potentially fluid, changing and promising.

Much of the organized religion has come under a canopy of Caesaropapism, with the prophetic voice stilled, and a comfortable accommodation to the nation's power substituted for the cry after justice, the psalm sung only to God. A distressing number of the clergy, finding their places in the corridors of power, give honor to American power instead of to God. They simplistically attack "godless communism" while equating America's role with God's, American righteousness with that of God. They offer worship at a national shrine, blasphemously doing this in the name of God.

No nation in the world can ever receive the worship that is intended only for God.

You are the salt of the earth; but if salt has lost its taste, how shall its saltness be restored? It is no longer good for anything except to be thrown out and trodden under foot by men.

You are the light of the world. A city set on a hill cannot be hid. Nor do men light a lamp and put it under a bushel, but on a stand, and it gives light to all in the house. Let your light so shine before men, that they may see your good works and give glory to your Father who is in heaven.

I accompanied a rabbi to Selma, Alabama, for the freedom march with Martin Luther King, Jr., in 1964. Our presence there could not be explained simplistically as "social action." For the rabbi, participation in the march was directly related to the teaching of the Torah that any suffering, anywhere in mankind, was therefore *his* suffering, *his* concern. His religious belief required this risk, witness and servanthood. For myself, marching in Selma was inseparable from my belief that God became man in Christ, and that I therefore express my love of Christ in the action of sharing love with my human brother. My religious belief required this manifestation of itself in action. My life in "the church" had to expand outside the four walls of a church building as well as the formal structure of a denomination, and include the Selmas of the world and humanistic revolution.

But I had to confront the complex question, What *is* the church?

Ivan Illich, the Catholic theologian-activist, has made

a helpful distinction between the church as "She" and the church as "It." He explained: "*She* is that surprise in the net, the pearl. She is the mystery, the kingdom among us. . . . *It*, however, is the institution, the temporary incarnational form. I can talk about It only in sociological terms. I've never had trouble creating factions and dissent toward the Church as It." Within Illich's defined context I find that my own commitment is not to "It," the establishment church, but rather to "She," the essential church. The essential church, linked so closely to the impulse of the humanistic revolution, is an indissoluble part of my flesh and dreams, blood and vision.

7

More and more people committed to the humanistic revolution have been engaged in a disturbing struggle as they seriously and responsibly try to decide what to *do* about the institutional church. It is a question of vast importance, sociopolitically as well as religiously, because the church's power, especially through interlocking institutions, affects the entire society.

It has seemed to me that there might be three loosely defined choices.

First, one might remain inside (or enter) the establishment church. There may be a chance to work for change within existing structures, bringing them closer to the spirit of the humanistic revolution. It is possible that one is "saving" what is best about religion by staying in. After all, isn't the establishment church the vessel of those truths that finally undergird the essential church? If one stayed in and struggled, maybe the ship would not sink.

On the other hand, there is a growing sense of futility about the establishment church when one becomes aware of the gimmicks it employs to rouse the troops, get money, create a bright, new image—but without its changing in any real sense. The institutional church seems to involve itself endlessly in a careful study of the wrong questions. It tries to make itself "relevant" to "modern man." Public-relations men and women hover in the wings to rush news of its latest panaceas and projects to an increasingly indifferent public. The establishment church, trapped in its self-made armada, uses coffeehouses, minorities, women, youth, social issues and the arts for the sake of its own "relevant" image, seldom being interested in people and movements for their own sake and fulfillment. "The sad truth is that the church *cannot* be the metainstitution our world needs to instruct us in festivity, to open us to fantasy, to call us to tomorrow, or to enlarge our petty definitions of reality," Harvey Cox wrote in *The Feast of Fools*. "It cannot be for only one reason: the church is not the church." The chasm between the establishment church's rhetoric about social issues, on the one hand, and its motives and actions, on the other, is too wide for mortal sight to span it.

In the long run, perhaps the most tragic of the establishment church's failures is its loss of the capacity to worship. This vacuum exists alongside the compelling spiritual hunger and thirst of many people, including youths who increasingly express a need of emotionally and intellectually acceptable rituals to punctuate life, pointing to the place of mystery in a highly pragmatic, technological society.

A Jewish student told me about her participation in a liberated church on her campus. Approximately forty students belonged to the loosely structured worship community, which contained Roman Catholics, Protestants, Jews and agnostics. Weekly holy communion consisted of vodka and cookies. "I still go every Friday night to a synagogue service," the student told me. "It's stiff and formal. If you accidentally touched somebody, he'd probably scream. All they do is worship God. But in our underground church, when we pass communion around we reach out and touch each other. We want physical as well as spiritual or mental contact. And we need it with each other. Anyhow, isn't God in us and here with us? Why do people always put God up in the sky or behind an altar in a church?"

In line with the burgeoning Women's Liberation movement, a nonordained woman—frequently a Roman Catholic—is asked to give the prayer of consecration in a "liberation mass," although many priests may be present. Confession can be an outpouring of many voices. Everybody present is given a chance to speak whatever is on his mind. People stand, or sit, in a circle. A growing number of pople are looking from the West toward Eastern spiritual experience. "The missionaries should have listened a lot more and learned about the native religions instead of trying to convert everybody to Christianity," a student told me.

The decreasing number of students who remain a part

of denominational religious structures tend to regard experiment as their norm. Their "rock masses" utilize psychedelic lights, musicians, vestments of their own making, incense, chants and improvised words. At one such mass, held in the chapel of an Ivy League university, students were passing the consecrated bread from hand to hand. Instead of wafers, a freshly baked French bread was used. "The Body of our Lord Jesus Christ," a student said, shoving a handful of damp dough into my nostrils and mouth. Many people would find this incident sacrilegious. For the students involved in it, the moment was a holy one. It involved a totality of feeling with all the senses. It was not circumspect or traditionally proper, but radically improvised and highly spontaneous.

Speaking for myself, I have seldom participated in institutional public worship in recent years when I have felt a sense of integrity regarding its existence. I cannot accept "worship" that is anti-worship, that is to say, deadened to holy impulse and choreographed in such a stilted (even caricatured) way as to exclude spontaneity, the free action of the Holy Spirit of God working in the participants. I have tried to comat this deadness.

In particular, I remember two worship services that were planned to point toward mystery and the recognition of spiritual hunger among the assembled people. Both services represented the combined efforts of vastly different people who came together for the purpose of what each individual defined as worship.

The first was held in the National Cathedral in Washington, D.C., on August 4, 1965. "It was a liturgy of the Word, and the words were 'freedom' and 'human dignity' and 'justice' and 'fraternal love.' . . . The vast cathedral was packed on Sunday night almost a half-hour before the scheduled program," *Liturgy* reported later. "A simple, square stage had been erected in the crossing, and it was casually filled with young people of many colors, sitting, sprawled, waiting to sing. The soaring, carved stone pulpit was filled, too, at its lectern and all the way down its steps to the choir." The singing of the congregation alternated with individual artists accompanying themselves on guitars. When the lights dimmed, a shoeshine box was seen in the center of the improvised stage; a play that I had written about black liberation, *Boy*, was performed by black actors who came from New York. Finally I climbed into the pulpit to preach the sermon. Young men and women, black and white, crowded into the large stone pulpit, where they stood shoulder to shoulder with me. Afterward the ritual singing of the people—hands clasped, bodies swaying—was confession of sins and benediction.

The second worship service also took place in Washington, D.C., three years later, sponsored by Clergy and Laymen Concerned About Vietnam. I was asked to open it with meditations and prayers. A student stood alongside me in front of the congregation, providing strummed accompaniment on his guitar when he felt moved by particular words. I closed with two meditations from my book *Free to Live, Free to Die*.

Isn't the siren blowing longer than usual this time, doesn't it seem to have lost control? Are the bombers only ten minutes away? Are the submarines surfacing on both coasts; has our radar been knocked out? . . . Do you suppose we're really going to *die*?

. . . .

A smokestack means burned bodies. A freight train moving along the tracks means people being transported like cattle to a concentration camp. . . . A whip means being lashed to a post, hands tied together in an upward position, while the hot leather (one, two, three times—twenty-one, twenty-two, twenty-three times) draws circles of blood on one's back—and screams from deep within one's self—and a satisfied response from hard-working torturers. . . . At least, that is what these things mean to some people.

I was touched by the written response of a Jewish student attending the worship service, for it provided a perspective of the event outside of my own experience as I continued to struggle with the meaning of worship and its possibilities within my own life.

I was battered by dreadful feelings during this worship, and yet a strange harmony emerged, a fellowship of anguish and commitment. The words bit into me, and I wept to hear of beauty and sweetness, bombs, fire, and God, are you with us? We who are silent and comfortable, do we call loud enough that you answer? God, I cannot remain alone; we stand by and watch the trains going to Auschwitz; the Vietnamese are dying and we rest in the evening. Will the bombs come closer? I felt the love of God surging through the preservation of human love.

I have spent many hours in reflection and sober

thought about these two worship services. Neither one seemed to be mere empty ritual or a superficial religious coating for the establishment's unchanged and structured exercise of power. Since the second worship service in Washington, D.C., I have drifted farther and farther from institutional church worship, with its unchanged rhythms (as if it did not hear the voices crying out in this age) and its seeming obsession with its own self-perpetuation.

Giving the establishment church more infusions to prolong its life seems to delay, if not prevent, its possibly necessary death. Must not death precede resurrection? This means genuinely new life as contrasted with mere renewal. Yet one cannot romantically indulge an image of a single death—that is, the image of instant revolution. This is antithetical to the moral concept of continuing and present revolution. It fails to comprehend the necessity of continuing and related "deaths," for an individual or an institution, if authentic new life is sought. Of course, it will not be new life; it will mean new lives, new living.

For people who are engaged in a struggle as they try to decide what to do about the institutional church, there appears to be a second type of alternative: one might join a liberated-primitive church. Or start one. A poet wrote me to describe his experience in such a church:

Five weeks ago I was invited to read at a poetry festival. The audience was mixed sexually, chronologically and educationally. Before the reading I still possessed my long-held belief that contemporary organized churchianity closely resembled the well-known description "standing absolutely motionless at a slight angle to the universe." However we were asked by the director of the evening to stay for coffee. I accepted. The idea of questions?????? I was positively flattered. No one had ever done much after a poetry reading except nod a few times and mutter yes! yes!, and please don't get mud on the rug on the way out.

But this group was different. They had listened and now wanted to probe. I was more than willing. They referred to *the religious content* of my poetry. I was completely stunned. And my first reaction was to deny. However, this group saw a whole new meaning to "religious." I learned that night the line of demarcation is no longer set by any chronological age when one passes from the ideal (Christian) to the pragmatic (an overdose of cynicism). If only the freedom of thought and enthusiasm of this group could be tapped or at least get outsiders to plug in. Suddenly I could smell the dank cellar smell that the early Christians could perceive in their underground meeting places. Here was truth and love.

I too was tired (as you and others like you) of programed one-bean-supper-social-a-week-religion. Tired of images of a tired Jesus, a defeated Jesus on a tower of wood. Tired of wondering how the keepers of the word had allowed Jesus to be buried under piles of hymn books turned brown from a kind of spiritual illiteracy. How did it come to pass that the vital breathing, vibrant social radical that was Jesus was hidden behind stained-glass windows and pious amens blocking out the world that he walked in as a man? I learned that night that Jesus was not dead but had climbed down from that marble pedestal and left the church to make it in the streets. That night, that discussion, that group of people with an idea to follow the communal spirit of love, have left their mark on me and they will not let me rest.

Yes. But one must subject to careful scrutiny, and a cooler mood sure to follow, the enthusiasm of this letter too. Jesus made it in the streets in the *first* place, and he was both tired and defeated; the acceptance of his resurrection, without holding in tension the tiredness and the crucifixion, is altogether to miss the point of Christianity. History is filled with stories of "that group of people with an idea to follow the communal spirit of love." So any new group needs to comprehend the history of institutional corruption, the stirrings of self-interest against altruistic idealism, and the ever-present factors of moral strain within all persons and movements, as it tries simply to follow Jesus in the streets. If it indeed follows Jesus—in the streets and elsewhere—it should do so with a keen awareness of history that mellows self-righteousness and keeps any group on guard against its mixed motives.

The problems of sectarianism are present in the liberated-primitive churches: a tendency to feel self-righteous and "persecuted," a hint of paranoia, emergence of a new elite with its own dogmatic traditions and "in" group, the lack of a sense of history and one's own place in it, sadly taking oneself too seriously and—linked to this—sacrificing humor even while perhaps holding onto joy. What of religious needs? One finds liberation-primitive church people coming back to the establishment church for a funeral, a wedding, or at a time of national crisis. Why? Certainly it may be partly out of habit. But it may also illustrate that the liberated church has not cut deeply enough, after all; maybe its new patterns simply obscure old forms. If so, some people feel more comfortable, under stress, with the familiarity of old patterns.

Liberation-primitive churches need to face the possibility that they may have overstressed social involvement (as a reaction to virtually none at all), while not truly meeting the profound religious needs of many people. A lot of social activists are interested in *religion*. However, they find that the churches, including the liberated ones, do not have it and therefore cannot offer it. So some of these people are taking up the occult or else resigning themselves to the fact that their religious needs conceivably cannot be met.

Of course, one might get out of the church. Stop the church, I want to get off. One may honestly feel, paradoxically, that the church is more truly itself out in the world—outside what is called "the church." This view was expressed to me in a letter I received from a Protestant divinity student.

I've got a problem [he wrote]. I'm drifting, I mean really drifting. And that's something I hate. I feel like packing up my bags and leaving. I want to help people, and I think I might want to do it as a minister, but I don't want to fight churchianity for the rest of my life. Like my roommate said (who shares many of the same confusions I do), he learns more from his atheist artist friends about how to be a Christian than from the stuff they throw at us here in the divinity school. Whenever I try to pin someone down to a discussion about some matter of personal faith, I get told that I have to consider all the teleological, certainly existential, and perhaps even ontological presuppositions of what I'm going to say. I once had someone tell me I've got a real epistemological hang-up. I told him to kiss off—it was one of my more courageous moments in the seminary—and then I felt bad.

I don't get hung-up on things like was there really a Virgin Birth. Virgin Births are kind of rare nowadays, so I really couldn't care less. (If I were in a counseling situation, I doubt if some chick would come to me with *that* kind of a problem.) I don't want to have to fight churchianity. I just want to tell people to love one another. That's all. But I don't think they'll let me do it in the ministry. They're more interested in answers for their goddam questions about life. They're so busy trying to find answers, intellectually that is, that the world goes by in the meantime and goes on suffering while they try to figure out what to do about it to their intellectual satisfaction. I would crap in my pants if I were in some parish as an assistant minister, if there was a big turnout for some discussion about "faith" or "grace" or all those other words I don't understand, and zero turnout for a discussion of race, like race relations in the school around the corner.

But the tendency to use religion as a primary means of avoiding confrontation with God is older than the hills. The seminarian is going to run into all the problems that he has mentioned in his letter. He will also run into them, in one form or another, in neighborhood community organization, a university school of social work, a narcotics counseling agency, or as a teacher in a high school. "Churchianity" is simply *one* form of institutionalization. His poignant plea—"I just want to tell people to love one another. That's all"—could be entitled Famous Last Words. The struggle to comprehend love, so that one does not commit murder in its very name, requires relationships with other people (institution) and a constant process of growing self-knowledge (education).

205

Getting out of the church might help one to work more creatively, not only with other people in helping them to solve their problems but also with self-identity—"priest," "minister," "layman," "laywoman," "sister" and/or human being? Yet how self-destructive might leaving the church prove to be, if one felt an isolation from roots? One might have a tendency to move into a jungle of subjective definitions, losing all sense of a greater, cohesive community. (I sense a terrible identity crisis in various men and women who are culture celebrities for the sole reason that they are ex-priests, ex-nuns, ex-bishops or ex-ministers. Their restlessness communicates itself fiercely. Often what they write and say is flat and empty.) Finally, in the act of leaving the church, one might never consciously find it again. A number of people, of course, may not want to find it.

But there is another question that must be faced. Is not "leaving the church" socially and existentially irresponsible for a person committed to the humanistic revolution? Or is one seriously attempting to grapple with the enormous power concentration of the institutional church, as an instrument of society, by spending one's time and energies in the development of new communal structures for a counterculture?

I can scarcely survive as a human being in the establishment church as it is presently constituted. Its schizophrenia heightens my own, its relentless commitment to the status quo wars with my biblical understanding of Jesus, its bureaucracy makes the postal system look avant-garde, and its ceremonies of celebration seem dry and joyless. On the other hand, I have learned to discern moral ambiguities in all men (including myself), all movements and institutions. This includes the liberated-primitive churches. I can respond to many decent intentions, Judeo-Christian-humanistic motivations, and examples of community and spiritual affirmations in this movement, but doubt that I can find my lasting home in it. It has new leaders (even heroes), press releases, schisms, social-political alliances, fund-raising efforts, conventions—and history repeats itself as yet another establishment is born.

The humanistic revolution will itself pull me first in one direction, then in another, as I struggle with the meaning of life style, honesty and, yes, discipleship. Where should I *put* my life? I shall have to ask that question again and again and again. Old answers, too long accepted even as a revolutionary stance, result simply in putrefaction.

For example, it is the reasoned opinion of many distinguished scientists that mankind now faces the possibility of a collective doom. In an interview (March 15, 1971) in *The New York Times*, Jacques Monod, the molecular biologist who shared a 1965 Nobel Prize in medicine, warned that human life on earth may not survive much later than 2050 unless a stable-state society can be achieved along with the destruction of nuclear stockpiles. However, he commented: "We have no right to have no hope, because if we have no hope, there is no hope." This points toward a prophetic and pastoral function of religion during a period when a presently unprepared mass of people may have to witness the deterioration of life as they have known it as well as increasing omens of the finality of this very cycle of life. In addition to affirming reverence for life, religion could assist people to express service to others over personal aggrandizement, and a gentleness of life style in the place of an aggression that would only accelerate chaos and doom. Circumstance and the onrush of events outside its own structured existence may force religion to accept a function of centrality in people's lives.

New forms of religious life are deeply significant for a people rooted in the Judeo-Christian heritage. Outward and visible signs of inner and spiritual meaning (sacraments) concern birth, love, mating, work, play, war, peace, ideals and death. They evoke moods of celebration, sacrifice, rage, community, acceptance, struggle and mystery. The ritual, or punctuation, of the main events in our lives provides a necessary rhythm and sense of movement. Without rituals we perish. On the one hand, I must await new forms of religious life to emerge; on the other, I must cooperate with their emergence, even in some instances understanding how this creative contribution will take place in my own life and experience. As Sam Keen wrote in *To a Dancing God*, "If I am to rediscover the holy, it must be in *my* biography and not in the history of Israel." Yet I should realize that with their emergence some new forms may at least resemble old ones, while the establishment church, as well as offshoot religious movements, can give birth to new forms in the action of creative tension.

I liked some things that were said in a preparatory statement for an Easter 1970 gathering of 2,500 young people from thirty-five different countries and five continents at the Taizé Community in France. It was discovered that "there exists a thirst for God, and at the same time the will to advance in the service of humanity." Where there was an understanding of Christ, "he is above all a life." There was interest in a church that is "creator." The youths desired a step to set free their energies, "that prepares within them a burst of creativity to make the earth fit to live in." It was felt that the southern continents made the essential contribution to the meeting, with Latin-American and Afro-Asiatic youths expressing central themes. It was announced that Jesus is preparing a springtime of the church that will become "devoid of means of power, ready to share with all, a place of visible communion for all humanity."

Without such a vision of new life, with whatever new forms of religious expression that it brings, the humanistic revolution is ground into dust and people cry out in the despair of dehumanized existence.

The vital life of the essential church is a major source of vision and sustenance for the humanistic revolution. Indeed, it is a task of the essential church to penetrate the life of the institutional church, reminding it of the moral difference between standing on the side of life and standing on the side of death.

It was evident, even a decade ago, that the institutional church was moving into a period of extraordinary vitality and controversy. On the TV talk shows, as bright lights manufactured sweat and cameras turned faster than the national conscience, fad prophets were announcing that "the church is dead." Yet an investments or automotive executive, creasing his newspaper in the smoke-filled den of a commuter's train, was as susceptible to fury or tension, at the mere mention of yet another church controversy, as a Roman-collared activist on a picket line or a pipe-biting bishop.

The essential church has never been more alive.

Indeed, it is too alive, some will argue. Why, they plaintively ask, can't it be subdued, respectable, prayerful, and, damn it, "religious"? All this social action marked by churchmen's involvement in poverty, sanctuary for men opposed to war, the sex revolution, black power and Vietnam. Good heavens, it's dastardly, economically unsound, and unfaithful to the blond, blue-eyed Jesus whose eyes always turned heavenward and who died, as we all know, peacefully in his bed.

As reporters of news magazines used to go around Hollywood, Paris and Washington inquiring, "What is so-and-so *really* like?," now a focus of hard concentration has come to rest on that unlikeliest of institutions, the church. Many people are asking "What *is* it? What is its *real* nature? What, for God's sake, is it supposed to *do*?" One fact is indisputable: the image of "religion" has changed. Pope John has come and gone, pumping hardy peasant blood into dry arteries. Rabbis have lived in Mississippi "freedom houses." Dietrich Bonhoeffer, hanged in a Nazi prison, raised a haunting question about "religionless Christianity." French worker-priests and other modern prophets have fused "the sacred" and "the secular." Clergymen have been joined by nonordained men and women acting out of religious conviction as sociopolitical protesters and resisters; many have been tried and jailed. One of these, Marjorie Melville (formerly Sister Marian Peter, who worked as a teaching nun in Guatemala), wrote in *Whose Heaven, Whose Earth?*:

In some extraordinary way I came to realize as never before that Christ *is* my living brother— He *is* the poor child in Castañás who needs food and medicine and water and wants to learn to read. Christ is not merely *in* him, He *is* the Indian who lives nearly starving and tries to grow some corn on a tiny plot on a hillside. He *is* the peasant leader who dares to resist the plantation owner and is beaten and killed. . . . Suddenly, I understood. And my literal, geographical concept of the Kingdom of Heaven and the Lake of Eternal Fire fell away before the onset of this new revelation: The real Heaven is a state of communion, of compassion and loving concern, with all our brothers and sisters, all of them incarnations of the Living Christ; the real Hell is a state of alienation, a being out of communion with yourself and with other people and with God, distrustful, competitive, prejudiced, seeing others as things, sources of profit and gratification only. This was a completely new insight to me, and I was thrilled with its meaning. I saw Christ struggling to be born in other faces.

The establishment's ecumenical movement spawned the postecumenical movement of the liberated primitive or underground churches. A new breed of Christians learned to laugh without bitterness at denominational quixotism, sexual legalisms, the edifice complex (the term had already become a cliché), Wizard-of-Oz leadership hiding within multimillion-dollar "headquarters," prayer as magic, "GUILT" in neon signs, and religious observances separated from life in that bizarre cultural hangover of a Sunday holy hour.

The church is always healthiest when it is responding, in genuine crisis and controversy, to honest tensions in the life of the world. I recall a bishop saying, "I have two types of clergy in my diocese, the disturbed and the dead. I hope that I will remain always one of the disturbed." A number of disturbed clergy and laymen are moving close together in a new life style that disrupts the old caste system separating them. An alive church will increasingly find its altar out on Main Street, its holiest people ordinary men and women who care about other people (and so, about God), and its "social action" placing its own body on the line, inseparable from the love it is always talking about in pulpits. A public demonstration is a good thing to jar a pickled conscience. But really effective social action (obedience to the gospel) is ongoing, steady, localized work rooted in such realities as "salvation" of education, housing, jobs, peace, politics and breaking down ghetto walls. The establishment church has known bleak, bad days in recent memory. It kept insanely silent as human bodies were fed to Auschwitz. More recently, it has had considerably more to say—in neat, professionally trimmed publicity handouts—about Thanksgiving, Christmas, Lent and Easter than about Hiroshima, napalm, the draft, Chicano pride in identity, black liberation, or casualty lists—on *both* sides.

Such tensions! On the one hand, the establishment church is the locus of those Sunday newspaper society wedding accounts; this a part of its being the place where the establishment marries, baptizes and buries, but virtually never conceives. On the other hand, the essential church is the continuing movement that shattered the

peace of a Peter, a Paul, a Francis, a Luther, a Kierke-
gaard, a Unamuno, a Marx and a Hammarskjöld. Success
seems to be coming to the church. Not by publicity-
measured real-estate construction, vaulted cathedrals, or
power structure prelates and evangelists who are "in"
with the government and politicians. The success symbol
of sacrifice and brotherhood becomes ever more central
to the experience of haunted contemporary men and
women who seek self-possession amid the accouterments
of affluence, a sign of personal identity in the cloverleaf
of technology, and communion with other people instead
of coexistence with posthumans who have been trans-
lated into machines.

At this crucial moment religious complacency is a
buried fantasy. The essential church—pockets of pilgrims
who have communion with each other in dispersion, and
experience-heightened hope in sadness—comprehends
that it must be ready to die, in this generation, celebrating new life in the person of the Jesus whom it calls
lord and brother. Even the militant, activist, sometimes
frightening reformers—invariably seen as cultural anti-
heroes—are caught in an anguished fear they seldom communicate to sophisticated newsmen and impersonal TV
cameras. Their fear is that they may be acting out of
"self-righteousness," which has replaced "paternalism"
as the current most damning word.

All in all—and despite bloodstains, wasteland rhetoric and racking strains that shatter lives—the essential
church, as a companion of the humanistic revolution, is
passionately alive, embarrassingly well (in light, that is,
of the various seers' prognostications about its demise)

and living in a moon-drenched world of sensitive, crazy, changing and growing people. These people do not hear the majestic, traditionally martial strains celebrating the divine Hero in regally imperial glory and establishment power. Instead there is quiet celebration of the life, death and resurrection of Jesus, the anti-hero of his own time, the brother and servant who died on the cross in God's identification with human injustice, suffering, failure and hope.

8

The humanistic revolution begins with one's own life, which always stands in need of transformation from egoism and self-interest. Authentic identity is of essential importance in the humanistic revolution, which is concerned essentially with changing the quality of life. Playing a calculated role, even if it should contribute to the "success" of a meritorious cause, must be seen as an indication of corruption and anti-humanism.

Virtually everybody possesses roles and images that are casually sewn into the fabric of a family, a neighborhood, a church, a university, a business, or a racial-ethnic category. Then a social cause or popular movement raises up personalities in the guise of leaders and even heroes. Soon the inevitable transformation into image occurs. Later, when people meet an idol, they "know" the idol, expecting it to conform to its image requirements. They have little or no interest in establishing a genuine relationship with the man or woman who exists beneath the image's frowns and folds, smiles and creases. Their emotional needs are related to the idol.

As we are surrounded by deceptive appearances of revolution, religion, protest and leisure, so publicly honored and exalted heroes may be manufactured public-relations products, while many men and women possessing genuine heroism remain strangers to fame.

A number of political, social and religious figures have ironically engineered entrapment in images of their own initial devising. This was done in order to trap the public also; afterward the charade is apparently guaranteed "success." Yet such "success" contains the pitfalls of deep unhappiness and horrifying isolation. One of the greatest of Hollywood's cinema stars told me her personal definition of success. In her experience, it was akin to holding a position on top of a flagpole. She said that one is all alone up there and must continually fight back those who climb up in an attempt to take over the top spot. One becomes dizzy at that height; the other persons, far below, begin to resemble mere ants. One loses all relationship with those persons, and the widening gulf distorts one's perspective. It is cold up there. The winds howl. The pole is greased. If one makes just one slip, the descent is all the way down to the bottom. People below hate the occupant of the top, hurling mud and rocks in an attempt to dislodge "the success."

Once the machinery of image-making is set in motion in order to create the myth of a success, it moves on inexorably. A barrage of propaganda, whether it is for a political campaign or a book, a person or an institution, can destroy the reality of truth in harsh assertion of image.

Images, in place of people, are henceforth interviewed by the mass media.

The human experience with the matter of heroes has been a devastating one in recent years. Men possessing steady access to the mass media have become our simulated heroes. Quite aside from what they did or did not say or personify, it was command of televison time, print space, the microphone, the loudspeaker, and the intense interest generated by these, that stamped them. Yet their altogether obvious fabrication loudly trumpeted itself.

There were several deadly blows dealt the hero business. Several years ago Americans learned that one of their own young men shot down by the Russians ("If he was patriotic, why didn't he commit suicide?") was *a spy*. Then American fighting men were accused of participating in a massacre ("American soldiers would not do that"), shooting down old men, women and children. Astronauts came into the public consciousness, and for a brief moment footsteps on the moon were framed in what resembled a luminous stage setting for *Waiting for Godot*; then, it seemed mere moments afterward, an astronaut was a media pitchman delivering a gasoline commercial on television. Even the man in the moon had been demythologized.

This was not all. The white-haired old heroes lay exposed to demythologization. I will never forget the night in a London pub when an angry young British journalist told me that he was going to attack Albert Schweitzer in a book. Schweitzer, the mythical figure, the living legend, who had given his life for the sake of poor and deprived Africans. "Poppycock," said the journalist in impassioned tones. I was horrified. I could not believe my ears. However, the journalist went on to document his case that Schweitzer was capable of error. The exposé appeared in the world press. Its thesis was essentially accepted: Schweitzer, too, possessed clay feet, mixed motives, the capacity for bad judgment, and had on occasion made mistakes.

We should really turn away now from the concept of heroes, and in the very process of doing so, seek to discover (and permit) heroism within ourselves. This heroism needs to be small-scale, low-key, and built into existing human situations. There can be no more advancing against the enemy astride a warrior's charger, with a mighty sword in hand, to uphold purity and justice against decadence and tyranny. We have learned that the enemy is as much within as outside *ourselves*.

The vision of a related world and one's organic function in it has to be based on one's own character, personality, strengths and weaknesses, not on slavishly emulating other people, or especially their images that obscure realities. Heroism is not glamorous. It might be found in Camelot only if that were one's home town.

It is an irony that the sensitively humanistic civil-rights and peace movements ordained men and women to become images and then myths. Critics inside these movements correctly and often angrily pointed out how media-nurtured heroes in the decadence of a celebrity cult were antithetical to the cause of personal and corporate freedom. Yet even when these critics most bitterly railed against celebrities within the movement and the worship of "names," still an urgent call went out to have "a name" for *this* demonstration, "a well-known person" for *that* event. In a lesser sense, I was among those sometimes called on. In the caustic but justified words of a Chicago critic, I became "a Christian showboat." Writing in *Book Week*, Joel Wells of *The Critic* said in 1970 that I had been "in the news as much as any American clergyman with the possible exception of Billy Graham, James Pike and Cardinal Spellman." It was a situation of sad paradoxes, difficult moral ambiguities, and, on my own part at least, considerable personal pain.

For I am tired of all posturing, image conformities, justification by the media, and weary predictability of word, attitude and behavior. Any "star"—a politician, an evangelist, a business leader, a labor leader, a "minority spokesman," or even a local luminary—takes his assigned place in front of TV cameras and plays. One man employs the gestures he has practiced before mirrors to convey sincerity. Another subtly uses his body to insinuate dynamism and strength. Voice timbres warm as if suspended over a crackling fire. There are megalomaniacs for all seasons, these ranging from ruthless zealots of the avant-garde to crustaceous guardians-of-the-usual. Follow the leader—with his absurd ego trip, personal bank account, press agents, career manipulation and style. What might once have indeed been sincerity has become a co-opted packaged product.

I used to be able to follow the leader. I cannot do it any longer. I will work in a cause rooted in the humanistic revolution with someone qualified who is the first among equals—but cut the turned-on charisma, please, as well as the programmed chic.

218

It is equally impossible for me to play the leader, because I do not want any role, especially that one. There was a time when I played the role at least adequately. This was in the days when serious civil-rights and peace movement planning invariably stopped long enough to mimeograph a stack of fresh press releases, and everybody knew an event had not *happened* unless it was seen in print in *The New York Times*.

My own image requirements were stipulated in a photograph taken of me by Robert Frank that appeared first in *Mademoiselle* and later on the cover of the best seller *Are You Running With Me, Jesus?*: sophisticated but sincere, tense-eyed but with soul, a swinger but certainly on the saintly side. A lovely legend about me at that time had me sitting *every night* inside a coffeehouse or bar, wearing my slightly soiled white clerical collar, and ready for hard, hip, beautiful and *now* conversation. A story, perhaps apocryphal, described an earnest young Catholic chaplain in Detroit entering a coffeehouse, sitting down at a table, and immediately finding himself surrounded by students. One of them smiled and shook his hand. "Hi, Father Boyd," he said.

I came to realize that the image that had developed was a product wrapped up in shiny paper and tied with a silver-and-gold noose, albeit sprinkled with holy water. Gradually I came to understand how deeply immoral it is to turn people, including oneself, into a product—whether for General Motors or God, IBM or the Peace Corps, Time-Life or Jesus Christ. I stopped the image process, retraced certain steps, started off in certain new directions, and stayed wary. I was not that image—or *any* image. I was myself.

Ideally, I learned, an interview should reveal a human being. Yet both a writer and his subject may earnestly desire an honest interview, only to find themselves lost among distorted and mocking mirrors, strange parodies and wax-museum imagery. In the course of a public life over the past decade I have been interviewed—by newspaper reporters, scholars, theologians, student journalists, on the radio and in front of television cameras—more than one thousand times.

Looking into the eyes of my interviewers, I have invariably seen their image of myself on that particular occasion: an angry and slightly lunatic-fringe "freedom rider" or "peacenik," a noble and idealistic civil-rights and peace activist; a publicity-seeking and essentially immoral priest-critic of the church, an articulate and essentially moral priest-critic of the church; a vulgarly lucky best-selling author who should not be taken seriously as a writer, a professional and serious writer; an insincere man, a sincere man. Then the image has been interviewed. But I seriously doubt that I myself ever have been.

I came to know that some people waited to define me in a paragraph, a shrug or a smile; my motives and feelings were thereby reduced to mere dimensionless categories. One correspondent aroused comment with a remarkably quotable observation. "Trying to interview Father Boyd is like trying to kill mosquitoes with a sling-shot," he wrote in the Toronto *Globe and Mail*. What did he mean? Knowledge of how one appears to other people is sparse to the point of virtual nonexistence. Yet

I am like most other people in yearning to be known and having my motivations and actions understood by others. Maybe then one could feel loved.

Several years ago, when I was forty-five, I was moved by a kind of desperation to write the first part of my autobiography. Surely it would illuminate the inner plains of self (I reasoned at the outset) and serve to define, for others as well as myself, the person I am. Yet almost immediately after it was finished I found myself asking hard questions about what salient facts and essential truths might not have got into the book. An autobiography, I learned, is weighted down by quicksand. The impulse to achieve autobiographical honesty is not nearly so important as the ability really to communicate it. Malcolm X came closer than anyone I know.

I regard the book as a curiously flawed and fragmented work. Was I Malcolm Boyd, the subject, or Malcolm Boyd, the interviewer? How to take another person by the hand and say, "Here is where I stood," "This is how I felt," "Do you hear my heartbeat and laughter, can you discern my fear and the tears that are streaming down my face?" Of course, what is not understood between two people in any human relationship, whether presumably casual or profound, public or private, sadly stands between image and truth.

It is a significant contribution to the humanistic revolution whenever people can assert human identity in the place of complex presence of roles, masks, appearances that contradict truths, and heroic (or anti-heroic) postures.

How can one gauge the quality of one's own life? It is

necessary to examine this question carefully in an effort to understand the dynamics of self as well as enable a greater openness concerning one's nature and motives in relationships with other people. For the humanistic revolution crucially begins with one's own life. Struggling in a "cause" for human freedom is a lie if one refuses to open up one's life to fundamental change in solidarity with other people who share the search for discovery of identity as a matter of existential and political reality. Yet the compelling demands of solidarity must always yield to individual conscience as the very cornerstone of the humanistic revolution.

ABOUT THE AUTHOR

MALCOLM BOYD received international recognition on the publication in 1965 of *Are You Running With Me, Jesus?* A Guest Fellow at Yale in 1968-69, he has lectured at universities throughout the United States and Canada. He has long been identified with his involvement in the civil-rights and the peace movements. Boston University has established the Malcolm Boyd Collection, a permanent archive of the Episcopal priest-writer's letters and papers.